MODELS AND WORLD MAKING

MODELS AND WORLD MAKING
Bodies, Buildings, Black Boxes

Annabel Jane Wharton

University of Virginia Press • *Charlottesville and London*

University of Virginia Press
© 2021 by the Rector and Visitors of the University of Virginia
All rights reserved
Printed in the United States of America on acid-free paper

First published 2021

9 8 7 6 5 4 3 2 1

ISBN 978-0-8139-4698-6 (cloth)
ISBN 978-0-8139-4699-3 (paper)
ISBN 978-0-8139-4700-6 (ebook)

Library of Congress Cataloging-in-Publication Data is available for this title.

Cover illustrations (*clockwise from upper left*): Female reproductive system, from Andreas Vesalius, *De humani corporis fabrica libri septem* (Basileae: Ex officina Joannis Oporini, 1543), 378 (David M. Rubenstein Rare Book and Manuscript Library, Duke University); 3D glass molecular model created by Purpy Pupple, November 22, 2010 (Purpy Pupple—own work, CC BY-SA 3.0, https://commons.wikimedia.org/w/index.php?curid=12121577); "Weather Forecasting Factory" by Stephen Conlin, based on the description in "Weather Prediction by Numerical Process" by L. F. Richardson, Cambridge University Press, 1922, and on advice from Prof. John Byrne, Trinity College Dublin (Image: ink and watercolour © Stephen Conlin 1986, All Rights Reserved).

This book is dedicated to Kalman Bland, who was fully engaged in the project both pre- and postmortem. His death delayed its writing; his life enabled its making.

Looking down on the helpless model, which resembles a crab squashed on the beach, one can only admire Eisenman's success at this task [of demonstrating architecture's post-Holocaust role of symbolizing impotence].

—Richard Pommer, *Idea as Model*

CONTENTS

	Acknowledgments	xi
	Introduction: Argument	1
1	Unmanageable Models/Definition	7
2	Body Model/Science/History	23
3	Building Model/Architecture/Politics	54
4	Black Boxes	101
	Notes	121
	Bibliography	147
	Index	175

ACKNOWLEDGMENTS

MANY HAVE contributed to the slow evolution of *Models*. I am very grateful to the staff and referees of the National Humanities Center, who provided me time and support for research and writing as the Birkland Fellow of 2016–17. My home institution, Duke University, has been most generous in allowing me time away to think about models as the Vincent Scully Visiting Professor at the Yale School of Architecture and the Harry Porter Visiting Professor at the University of Virginia School of Architecture. The students in the graduate courses on model theory that I taught at Duke, Yale, and Virginia contributed greatly to my understanding of the subject.

The participants in interdisciplinary venues in which I presented preliminary work on the definition of models also facilitated its refinement: notably the De Marchi Economic History Colloquium and the Media Arts and Science Forum of the Levine Science Research Center at Duke. Similarly, the audiences at lectures that I was invited to give at the schools of architecture at Yale, North Carolina State, and Bilkent University in Ankara, as well at the University of Minnesota and Princeton University, were most helpful. My work on cadavers and early modern Holy Sepulchres was also first presented in invited lectures at the University of Virginia and Dumbarton Oaks in Washington, DC.

I have additionally benefited from extended discussions with model experts: Mary Morgan, economic historian at the London School of Economics, Derek Ehrman, lead programmer for Red Storm Entertainment (Ubisoft), David Levinthal, model artist and photographer. Peter Eisenman and Alan Plattus enriched my understanding of built space; Charles Sparkman and Chris Brasier refined my sense of the powers of BIM. Also essential to my work has been the access to models provided by those who curate them, notably Dora Thornton, curator of the Waddesdon Bequest and of Renaissance Europe at the British Museum, Gabriella Sorelli, director of the Museo Marino Marini in

Florence, and Yoram Tsafrir, former director of the Jewish National Library and longtime superintendent of the Model of Jerusalem. I am particularly grateful to Dr. Matthew Velkey, Dr. Daniel Schmitt, the five medical students of table 21 (Meg, Jackie, Jon, Steven, and Jessy), and Lucy, our cadaver, who opened with me the deeply affecting archive of the body in Duke's first-year gross anatomy course through the fall of 2018. And to Rebekah Hudson, John Garnham-Davies, and Mark Curwood of the Nottingham Repository Centre in England for an introduction to cadaver preparation and embalming. Friends in my neighborhood—Catherine Hart and Susan and Elliot Schaffer—tried, with limited success, to help me make parts of this book more accessible. Ásta and Dore Bowen, my comrades at the National Humanities Center, were wonderfully provocative interlocutors. My colleagues at Duke, Marc Brettler, Elizabeth Clark, Paul Jaskot, David Morgan, Mark Olson, Victoria Szabo, Sheila Dillon, and Augustus Wendall have offered both support and productive criticism. I am also grateful to the many commentators on bits of the project, among whom are Barbara Herrnstein Smith, Kevin Hoover, Meltem Gurel, Valeria Finucci, Larissa Carneiro, Dale Kinney, Kaylee Alexandra, Helmut Puff, Alexandra Masgras, David Turturo, Bruce Hancock, Patsy Vanags, Alan Griffiths, Robin Cormack, Mary Beard. Helping me with my translations and, more generally, with my thinking, were James Rives and Gigi Dillon. Contributing to the refinement of my arguments were the anonymous reviewers of the manuscript; greatly facilitating the process of publication were my editors at UVA Press, Boyd Zenner, Mark Mones, and Maura High. My greatest debt is to Kalman Bland. He shaped this study not only while he lived, but also after he died.

 A note on text recycling. An early version of my definition of models, presented at *"Imagined Forms, Modeling, and Material Culture,"* a conference organized by Martin Brueckner, Sandy Isenstadt, and Sarah Wasserman at the University of Delaware, appears in the conference proceedings, published by the University of Minnesota Press. In addition, the Church of the Holy Sepulchre is a central object in *Selling Jerusalem: Relics, Replicas, Theme Parks* (University of Chicago Press, 2006). That sanctuary's varied appropriations by the West from pre- to postmodernity (from London's twelfth-century Temple Church to the Holy Land Experience) provided the basis for an argument about the progressive commoditization of the sacred in Protestantized societies. In the present text, the same sites appear along with new ones to document historical shifts in model making and representation.

MODELS AND WORLD MAKING

INTRODUCTION
Argument

> "Model," in my view, is just a word for people who cannot spell "hypothesis."
> —DEREK AGER, *The New Catastrophism*

FROM ALGORITHMS and economic pie charts to Barbie dolls and video games, models are everywhere. As climate change models and pandemic maps now demonstrate with particular force, models are not only an integral part of our daily lives; they are also intimately involved in conditioning the future of our species. The power and ubiquity of models make them a crucial object of study.

Models' essential contribution to research is fully acknowledged in the physical and social sciences, where models are not only pervasively deployed in research and its evaluation but are themselves the subject of serious scrutiny. Critical interest in models in the arts and humanities has also emerged.[1] But the illimitable variety of models has discouraged the interdisciplinary investigation of models. Most model studies treat a single genre of model: mathematical, climatic, architectural, economic, literary. Scholarly examination of models in general, like Max Black's *Models and Metaphors*, Marx Wartofsky's *Models: Representation and the Scientific Understanding*, Reinhard Wendler's *Das Modell zwischen Kunst und Wissenschaft*, or the magisterial *Springer Handbook of Model-Based Science*, edited by Lorenzo Magnani and Tommaso Bertolotti (which defines "science" very broadly) are relatively rare.[2] This book contributes to that broader conversation about models by defining, historicizing, and politicizing them.

The structure of *Models and World Making* is simple. The first chapter, "Unmanageable Models/Definition," works to control models by defining them. Definitions generally assert our ability, through the power of language, to manage some small aspect of the world. An inclusive definition of models offers some sense of mastery over this particularly unruly form. The process of thinking through a definition of all models also reveals their strengths and weaknesses. It further suggests that characteristics conventionally attributed to certain model types are found, to a greater or lesser a degree, in all others. This definition thereby establishes commonalities between humanist and scientific models. The first part of my definition is derived from common language; the second part depends on the sophisticated investigations of models undertaken in the quantitative sciences. The resulting formulation certainly demonstrates how much humanists like myself might be taught about our own models by scientific ones. Nevertheless, a definition of "model" dependent exclusively on common language and on research in the sciences and social sciences remains incomplete. A humanist perspective supplements that definition in an effort to make it more effective.

That humanist perspective critically addresses disclaimers made by some scientists and social scientists about the history and politics of their models. I discussed my definition of models in a small conference of economists, one of whom insisted that his models were not historical. I asked if he thought that the Phillips-Newlyn model is historical. The Phillips-Newlyn Hydraulic Analogue Machine is an elaborate and cumbersome apparatus with pumps, basins, and tubes siphoning colored fluids. It appears so functional that it looks like it might have come from an old hospital (fig. 1). Without reading the labels (savings, income after taxes, consumption expenditure), no noneconomist would guess that it was built to model monetary flows and was housed in a mid-twentieth-century department of economics.[3] Similarly, when I presented my definition at a science faculty luncheon, a physicist insisted that his models were not political. I asked him about the sources of funding for his lab. All models are not only historical but also political, whether those politics are micro or macro.

My argument for the historicalness and the politicalness of models is offered in the form of dense histories of two very different model types: the enduring architectural model and the equally persistent scientific, medical body model, the cadaver. Both model types have rich histories; they are well documented visually as well as textually. Chapter 2, "Body Model/Science/History," treats the cadaver. Much

Fig. 1. Alban William Housego Phillips with his hydraulic analog model of monetary flow. (LSE Image Library, PA2284, ca. 1958)

has been written on the cadaver—learned descriptions of its dissection, exhibition, and abuse. Considerable research has also been published on the illustration of medical texts from antiquity to the present. Less thought has been given to the question of how the dramatic shifts in representation in the West relate to changes in the cadaver's social and material being, in its ontology or essence. Transformations in the visual renderings of the medical body model—from diagrammatic to hyperreal—contributed to modifications of the cadaver itself. The body dissected in third-century BCE Alexandria and the cadaver in the Duke University anatomy lab in 2020 are utterly different. Together, the modified body and its depictions offer insight into the historical synergies of knowledge production. Cadavers, with the help of fashion supermodels, offer a supplement to my initial definition: all models are historical.

If the cadaver is an unexpected site for exploring scientific models, architecture may seem an odd field in which to probe the politics of humanistic ones. In chapter 3, "Building Model/Architecture/Politics," I analyze a series of Western models made of the Church of the Holy Sepulchre, site of the burial of Jesus in Jerusalem. Those models include monumental commanderies of the Knights Templar, Alberti's Rucellai tomb in Florence, Franciscan olive wood replicas, an archaeological model of Herod's Jerusalem, and video game renderings in *Assassin's Creed*. This premodern to Anthropocene sequence of models of the same archetype map dramatic changes in the conception, construction, and function of architectural models as well as in the politics of their social performance. The shifts recorded in architectural models are analogous to those of the medical body model, nuancing an understanding of the character and implications of history for models: architectural models reinforce the recognition of models as historical markers of social transformation. Architectural models also manifest more clearly than do cadavers the political force of models. They suggest that while some models may be passive agents, others are aggressive, even dangerously ideological ones. These Holy Sepulchres provide the basis for a further extension of my initial definition: all models are political.

All model types change over time in how they represent their referents. For the sake of clarity, I have characterized models' distinct historical forms as premodern index, early modern icon, modern analog, and Anthropocene simulacrum. This scheme is, like any model or typology, a simplification and therefore a distortion of its object, but the labels flag significant chronological distinctions. Index, icon, analog, and simulacrum are different modes of signification and representation; those terms are defined as they make their appearance in the text. Premodern, early modern, modern, and Anthropocene are period names. Periodization (a symptom of modernity bred of eighteenth-century rationalism) is the politically and culturally conditioned practice of cutting history into chunks to make it more digestible.[4] It is a fiction that contributes to the (misleading) coherence of our narrations of the past. It divides Western history into a sequence of eras—familiarly, premodern (ancient and medieval), early modern (Renaissance), and modern—that are distinguished by their economic, social, and cultural particularities. "Modern," with its allegiances to nationalism, industrialization, paper money, and individualism, is no longer an appropriate descriptor of our own moment.[5] The dramatically changed political and technological conditions of the end of the twentieth and beginning of the twenty-first century have produced several sobriquets. Most of the labels proposed—postmodern, late modern, posthuman—defer to the canonical authority of the West's modernity.[6] Here I identify the present as the "Anthropocene," because it presents our age as diabolically distinct. It also goes beyond Western cultural naming: in addition to being global, "Anthropocene" is also geologically epochal.[7] Models not only bear the marks of the period in which they were made; they also, as critical tools of understanding, catalyze new ways of thinking and acting, contributing to the emergence of new cultural dominants. My comparative analysis suggests not only that architectural and medical models, and, by extension, all models, have more in common than has been assumed, but also that model making is intimately connected to world making.

Chapter 4, "Black Boxes," considers the political and social implications of contemporary computational models. Black boxes are instruments whose inputs we manipulate and whose outputs we interpret, but whose inner workings are beyond our comprehension. A "black box," not unlike Pandora's box, encloses dynamics that have an effect, but which are themselves a mystery. But in contrast to Pandora's box, black boxes don't have to be opened to make us miserable. Black boxes are generally metaphorical (like computers for most of us). Now, however, as increasingly complex products of artificial intelligence fashioned by teams of scientists on a variety of platforms, black boxes (like programs predicting climate change) may also be genuinely impenetrable. Models produced by means no longer fully under human control may get out of hand. Considered here are the threats that opaque computational models hold not only for the central subjects of this study, buildings and bodies, but for the world. Perils range from abominable landscapes to ethical adventurism. Discussion of models' coupling with black boxes reinforces the importance of politics to the definition of model by nuancing an understanding of the model's moral compass.

Black boxes, as enigmatic devices, produce models that require particularly careful explanations. For example, climate change models, which are generated by black boxes, have suffered from intentional misinterpretations made by climate change deniers. Black boxes, consequently, are powerful advocates of the final claim of my definition: all models are entangled in discourse. If good model-makers, whether they are scientists, social scientists, humanists, or artists, embrace a broader understanding of their powerful products as autonomous historical and political agents, they may shape both their models and their discourses a bit differently. After all, not only are models, like the rest of us, enmeshed in discourse, history, and politics, but now humans are entrapped in models.

1
Unmanageable Models/Definition

> Few terms are used in popular and scientific discourse more promiscuously than "model." A model is something to be admired or emulated, a pattern, a case in point, a type, a prototype, a specimen, a mock-up, a mathematical description—almost anything from a naked blonde to a quadratic equation—and may bear to what it models almost any relation of symbolization. . . . "Model" might well be dispensed with in all these cases in favor of less ambiguous and more informative terms.
>
> —NELSON GOODMAN, *Languages of Art*

MODELS ARE out of control. From engineered mice and "naked blondes" to BIM (building information modeling) screens and set theoretic structures, models are profligate, if not, as Nelson Goodman suggests, "promiscuous."[1] Models are increasingly complex and powerful. With the digitalization of the world, models have come to dominate science, technology, and consequently our lives.[2] In an effort to exert a modicum of discipline over these unruly creatures, I offer a short, inclusive definition of models.[3] This definition imposes a certain conceptual order on models, curbing their incoherence. Although there is no restricting their power, the process of defining models reveals something of their character. Getting to know models is rather like getting to know humans: it provides you with a comforting sense of familiarity that may be empowering, though it is often delusional; it allows you to make critical interventions, though without much confidence in your criticisms' effectiveness.

Model in Common Sense and Common Language

Members of an educated audience readily recognize some features that are common to all models. Those broadly acknowledged characteristics provide the basis for my definition. Most fundamentally: *all models have referents.* There is no such thing as a model without something to which it refers.[4] Both the model and its referent may take an infinite variety of forms. As Marx Wartofsky has observed, "Anything can be a model of anything else."[5] Models can be conceptual, material, or imaginary. An alphanumeric expression may be a model for a theory; a pig may be (unfairly) a model for certain bad human behaviors; a fantasy castle can be a model of a (man's) home. A model's referent is equally free of any formal restraint. A shadow in a cave may be a model of the Platonic Idea; billiard balls may be a model of a law in physics; Snow White's castle in Disneyland may be (unfortunately) the model of a little girl's fantasy future.

Models take an infinite variety of forms and have an infinite range of referents. They also have a vast array of ways of relating to those referents. Figure 2 suggests a few of the various means by which a model might connect with its referent—Goodman's "relation of symbolization" (fig. 2).[6] A model can relate to its referent mimetically or iconically. An *icon* (εἰκών), for semiologists as well as for the Ancient Greeks, is an image: an icon conveys its meaning through visual resemblance. ☺ is an icon signifying pleasure. Scale models, like toy trucks, relate to real trucks by looking like them. Visual resemblance also describes the relationship between a netsuke dragon and its imaginary inspiration or between a wooden panel on which Jesus is depicted and God's second self. The connection here between the model and its referent depends on the replication of the archetype's external properties, whether that archetype exists in the world or in the mind. Mimetic correspondence is realized by an assortment of means—mirrors, cameras, mathematical measurements, graphic depictions, thick descriptions, and the like.

A model can also relate to its referent abstractly or symbolically, that is, by a form that is understood through convention or instruction. An abstract or symbolic model has no descriptive or physical connection to its referent. The academic community has been trained to recognize the © in the front matter of this book as staking the claim of the University of Virginia Press to the book's intellectual content. An equation or an algorithm is an alphanumeric construction that stands in for a narrative proposition, theory, or phenomenon. A pie chart or a

A. Relates mimetically or iconically

$\dot{X}_i = f(X_i) + \sum_{j \to i} H(X_j, X_i)$
$i = 1, \ldots, 8$

B. Relates abstractly or symbolically

C. Relates symptomatically or inferentially

FIG. 2. A. Jerusalem, Altair at the Dome of the Rock in the video game *Assassin's Creed* (Ubisoft Montreal, 2007; *left*, screen capture by the author). B. Equation (*left*, from Pietro-Luciano Buono, "Models of Central Pattern Generators for Quadruped Locomotion: Secondary Gaits," *Journal of Mathematical Biology* 42 [2001]). (All other photographs—Dome of the Rock, running horse, paper place setting, screen capture from *Downtown Abbey*—public domain)

graph is a model for an economic condition or for fluctuations in the weather. All these models work abstractly or symbolically to convey the meaning of the object to which they refer.

Another means by which a model might relate to its referent is symptomatically, inferentially, or indexically.[7] How silverware is ordered is a symptom of acculturation. A host's arrangement of place settings for a dinner party offers a model of the cultural habits of his class and points to his social standing.[8] The program of a modern office building with its cubicles and corner executive suites modeled the hierarchy of corporate power.

These examples of models, cited to demonstrate the vast variety in their forms and their relationships, make an additional commonsense point about models: not only must a model have a referent, but it must also differ in some way from that referent. As Ludmilla Jordanova productively puts it, "'Model' is what can be called an incomplete concept in implying the existence of something else, by virtue of which the model makes sense."[9] A model is not a model of an object if it is identical with it—rather, it would then be a clone, a simulacrum, a double. The ways in which a model may differ from its referent are infinite, as varied as its referent's form and the means by which it relates to its referent. Many of those ways are obvious. Models conventionally differ from their referents by changes in their scale (usually, but not always, smaller), their complexity (usually, but not always, simpler), and/or their material form (usually, but not always, cheaper). A model is also always distinct from its referent in its way of being in the world: it serves a different function, it elicits different forms of attention, it lives and dies in a different way.[10]

This way-of-being-in-the-world distinction is demonstrated by an apparent exception to the proposition that models differ from their referents: the commodity model. In common language related to cars, guns, and mechanical parts, "model" promises that each object of that particular class is identical to all others. When you order an "iconic silver" 2021 Ford Mustang Mach-E you expect it to be identical to the model of an "iconic silver" 2021 Ford Mustang Mach-E appearing on the Ford Motors website. When a buyer orders a Zastava PAP M92 model semiautomatic pistol from the Delray Arms Company of Florida, he expects to receive a gun that looks and acts exactly like that used in the Paris massacre in 2015.[11] Etymology, however, reveals that this type of model references its prototypical mold, not other members of the same series.[12] "Model" is a variant emerging from the Latin masculine *modus* (measure, size), which is closely related to *modulus* (a standard unit of measurement). In Middle French *modus* was feminized to *mode* ("a collective manner of living or thinking proper to a country or age") and *modulus* to *modelle*. Another cognate circulating in late medieval English was *moldus* ("template used in building" or "hollow form for casting metal"). The meanings of these various forms of *modus* were commonly conflated in early modernity. Shakespeare has Ophelia describe Hamlet before his madness as "the glass of fashion and the mold of form" (*Hamlet*, 3.1.161). In the eighteenth century, Samuel Johnson clarified the final phrase as "the model by whom all endeavored to form themselves."[13]

An even more relevant demonstration of this model/mold ambiguity is offered by the distinguished English mathematician, astrologer, and antiquary John Dee (1527–1609) in his preface to *Euclid's Elements of Geometry*. There he discusses proportional systems from Vitruvius and Euclid that allow any particular thing to be scaled up or down:

> Now, any regular body; any Sphere; yea any Mixt Solid: and (that is more) Irregular Solides, may be made (in any proportion assigned) like unto the body, first given. Thus, of a *Manneken*, (as the *Dutch* Painters terme it) in the same *Symmetrie*, may a Giant be made; and that, with any gesture, by the Manneken used; and contrarywise. Now, may you, of any Mould, or Modell of a Ship, make one, of the same Mould (in any assigned proportion) bigger or lesser. Now, may you, of any Gunne, or little piece of ordinance, make an other, with the same *Symmetrie* (in all points) as great, and as little, as you will.[14]

In Dee's engaging discussion of reproduction, identicality, and scaling, the terms "mold" and "model" are treated as interchangeable. "Model" was regularly substituted for "mold" in descriptions of such premodern production processes as candle-, plate-, and horseshoe-making. However, "model" (used as a reference to a particular mold) became part of everyday language only with industrialization and the need to specify particularity in a commercial world where things were increasingly fungible. You don't need a model number for the kettle made for you by the local blacksmith or the spoon you carved from your ash tree; you need a model number to replace a failing part in your refrigerator. That part needs to come from a specific mold or archetype. A mold, like a model, is distinct from its referent/product. Most obviously, the mold is both prior to its referent and its inverse. The mold's way of being in the world is different from that of its referent. It serves a different function, elicits different forms of attention, and comes into and out of existence in a different manner. This ontological argument might apply to the isomorphic models of mathematical model theory, but I don't understand enough about mathematical model theory to know for sure.[15]

Another commonsense understanding of models: some are powerful and others are not. The strength or weakness of a model, like that of a human, depends on its integrity, its formal coherence, its particular social location, its effectiveness, and its luck. A model's relative strength is different from that a human, however, because it is significantly conditioned by its referent. The authority of a model depends to some degree on the status of its archetype. A strong referent certainly does not ensure the power of its model, but it may well contribute to it. The aura of the Dome of the Rock clings to its model. The Yale investment model was adopted by other universities, often disastrously, at least in part because Yale used it.[16] A model of DNA has standing because DNA is the chemical key to the human. An algorithmic model of a beautiful cantering horse is also beautiful, at least to those in mathematical biology (fig. 2B).[17]

The weakness or strength of the model agent depends only in part on the status of its referent. It is more peculiarly determined by the conditions of their relationship. In this text, "*strong*" describes a model that acts as a dominant subject that determines its weak object.[18] An architect's model, for example, may be expected to work as an archetype for the building to be constructed. The market may change to conform to a rhetorically powerful economic model made of it. Joan Smalls, supermodel, makes clothes look fabulous, though she makes women feel ungainly. There are also *weak* models. Weak models act like copies. Copies are always subordinate to their archetypes. However much fun it is to play with, a toy car is inevitably a weak model of the real thing. This distinction between weak and strong has much in common with Clifford Geertz's well-known distinction between "models of" (the rendering of complex things in "synoptic form" to make them apprehensible) and "models for" (synoptic renderings allowing the production of more complex things).[19] But my distinction between "weak" and "strong" is, critically, much less clear than that made between "of" and "for" by Geertz. The distinction between weak and strong captures a broader range of potential relations. It allows a fuller appreciation of a feature of models that is obvious once it is pointed out: models may shift between their weak and strong potentials. A Barbie doll, which is a weak copy of a supermodel, may well also act as a strong model, contributing directly to the eating disorder of her possessor. This oscillation of the model in relation to its referent gives the model its centrally important capacity to make its observers rethink the archetype.

From a foundation of common language come the tentative first two sentences of my definition of models:

A model is [a thing] *that has a referent (material, ideal, conceptual, imaginary, . . .) to which it adverts (mimetically, symbolically, symptomatically, inferentially, . . .), but from which it differs in significant ways (in its complexity, scale, material, function, way of being-in-the-world, . . .). In its relation to its referent, a model is weak or strong, sometimes oscillating between the two.*

Model in Science

"Thing" is bracketed in the first iteration of my definition because "thing" is an inadequate equivalent of model. "Thing" implies objecthood. As Bill Brown claims, "We begin to confront the thingness of objects when they stop working for us: when the drill breaks, when the car stalls, when the windows get filthy, when their flow within the circuits of production and distribution, consumption and exhibition, has been arrested, however momentarily."[20] "Thing" tends to be both too material and too inanimate to effectively signify "model." "Thing" doesn't readily admit ideas, like utopias, or graphic abstractions, like algorithms. "Thing" doesn't readily admit sentient beings, like the supermodels on fashion runways or the model mice in a scientist's laboratory. "Thing" does, however, bear with it a useful sense of an object's independence from its human observer.

Scientists and social scientists provide the basis for substituting "agent" for "thing" as a descriptor of "model." "Agent" appropriately emphasizes a model's autonomy while freeing it from the materiality or inertness of "thing." Indeed, agency allows "model" to assume its proper liveliness, warranting, for example, its ability to oscillate between strong and weak. The case for models' agency is effectively made by Margaret Morrison, a philosopher of science.[21] Models are, she claims, independent both of the world and of the particular theory about the world that they are designed to demonstrate. She convincingly argues that if models are going to act effectively, they must be distinct from the theories that inspired them and from the empirical data that they are attempting to more fully understand, explain, or reveal. From examples drawn largely from physics, Axel Gelfert similarly concludes that models "are not simply neutral tools that we use at will to represent aspects of the world around us; rather, they contribute new elements—which are neither to be found in the underlying 'fundamental theory' nor to be found in the empirical data—to the process of scientific inquiry and, by mediating between different types of user–model–world relations, enable the generation of new scientific knowledge."[22] The work of Bruno Latour, a French anthropologist and theoretician, pushes agency further, redefining the social to include objects as well as humans as active participants in its web.[23] Latour's description of an object's autonomous acts in the world allow Morrison and Gelfert's understanding of models' independence to be extended beyond their relation to theories and data. Indeed, once complete, models should be recognized as independent of their makers and their consumers—as children are independent of their parents or, perhaps less ambiguously, as buildings are independent of their architects.[24]

The agency that is ascribed to models by scientists and social scientists is not the agency of common language or of humanist philosophers. In those more familiar contexts, agency is exclusively human and deeply embedded in heavily freighted concepts of morality, intentionality, and free will. But Latour's agent, and the agent of my definition, is more like that of chemistry or business. In chemistry, an agent is merely a substance, but a substance that has a physical, chemical, or medicinal effect on proximate things. Intentions and consciousness might be ascribed to the humans that deploy such agents, but certainly not to the chemical agents themselves. In business, an agent is "a person [the agent] employed by another [the principal] to act for him."[25] If in chemistry, consciousness and intentionality are extraneous to agency, in business, agency also loses most of its ethical baggage. The agent of chemistry or business is less burdened and closer to its etymological roots than that of the humanities. "Agent" is derived from the Latin verb *agere:* "to lead or to set in motion." In treating *models* as agents, I am, as in chemistry, naming entities—whether spatial objects, abstract notations, sets of thought, or even human beings (like infants or drunk drivers)—that have an effect on their physical or mental environments without requiring of them any inkling of consciousness or intentionality. A model agent differs from a chemical agent in that its effects on its setting are much less predictable. The model agent is also like a business agent. It may be assigned tasks by its principal (maker, patron, or owner). But if and how those tasks are carried out is not contractually binding: a model's capacity to oscillate between weakness and strength in relation to its referent is symptomatic of its agency. However a principal might intend her model agent to act, she can never fully control its actual performance in the world. All architecture students have experienced this unruliness of models during studio critiques.

As independent objects in the world, models often outlive those who constructed them; models that survive over time continue to function, but often in altered ways dependent on their changed contexts. Models are different from fungible commodities. A tomato has a history, but it, like all other fungible commodities, loses that history along with all of its other particularities when it is processed into catsup by Heinz. In contrast, models have biographies that may, with some effort, be reconstructed. Models are autonomous agents, at least in so far as anything in the world is autonomous.

Scientific models reveal another essential aspect of all models. The model depicted in figure 2B is only a model for those in mathematical biology. If encountered out of context, this algorithm would not be recognized as a model by most humans. In other words, readers unfamiliar with mathematical biology have to take this algorithm to be a model on faith. In order to interpret a model in relation to its referent, it must be comprehensible. Physics equations, economic graphs, and even axonometric drawings may well not be accessible to those unfamiliar with their symbolic codes. That exegetes must understand the language of the models on which they comment is obviously the case with computational forms. But it is equally so with apparently more obvious examples. A nuanced reading of David Levinthal's ironic images of war, published in *Hitler Moves East: A Graphic Chronicle, 1941–1943*, for example, requires its interpreter to recognize that the figures are model toys and to know that model toys are ordinarily ludic objects (fig. 3).[26] To offer a valid interpretation of a model, a commentator must be conversant with the rules of the model type on which she remarks: she must be aware of its hermeneutic conventions.

Perhaps the most important aspect of a model identified and discussed by scientists is its truthlessness.[27] It is well established that models inevitably distort their referent by changes in its complexity, scale, material, function, and the like. As a consequence, the model inevitably deviates from the truth of the referent. The consensus among scientists and philosophers of science who think and write about

FIG. 3. David Levinthal, photograph from *Hitler Moves East*, 1975. (Courtesy of David Levinthal)

models is that models are fabrications in all of that word's senses. To the question "Can a model be true?" Karl Popper, the distinguished philosopher of science, answers:

> I do not think so. Any model, whether in physics or in the social sciences, must be an over-simplification. It must omit much, and it must overemphasize much. . . . It seems to be quite unavoidable in the construction of models, both in the natural and in the social sciences, that they over-simplify the facts, and thus do not represent the facts truly.[28]

More critical is Alain Badiou's observation: "The model does not administer any proof. It is not *constrained by a demonstrative process, but merely* confronted with the real. And so, if the model represents the truth of scientific work, this truth is never anything other than the best model."[29] Because the model is a consciously altered (usually highly simplified) version of its referent, "truth" cannot be claimed either for its own verisimilitude or for conclusions drawn from it about its referent. Richard Levins, a biomathematician, advises us that "models, while they are essential for understanding reality, should not be confused with that reality itself."[30] John Casti, a mathematician, observes, "Models are tools for reality organization, i.e., a tool for ordering experiences rather than a *description* of reality."[31] Isabelle Peschard, a philosopher of science, argues that empirical truth claims can be made about model data-generation, but not about the relation between the model and phenomena.[32] Kevin Clarke and David Primo, political scientists, summarize the scientific view: "If there is one thing that those who think deeply about models agree on, it is that models are actually not truth-apt."[33] "True model" is an expression like "true representation." By frustrating expectation (representations, like models, are never fully true), the locution emphasizes that the representation (or model) under consideration is more proximate to its referent than most representations (or models) are to theirs. The understanding of models as truthless has serious epistemological consequences for their work ethic.

The ways in which scientists and social scientists understand models suggests modifications and additions to my initial definition:

> A model is *an autonomous agent* that has a referent (material, ideal, conceptual, imaginary, . . .) to which it adverts (mimetically, symbolically, symptomatically, inferentially, . . .), but from which it differs in significant ways (in its complexity, scale, material, function, way of being-in-the-world, . . .). In its relation to its referent, a model is weak or strong, sometimes oscillating between the two. *A model assumes its interpreter's familiarity with its particular hermeneutic conventions. No model can ever licitly make truth claims.*

Work Ethic

Models are as diverse in their functions as they are in their forms. Something of the difficulty of offering a definitive list of model functions is suggested by a selection of such inventories. Leo Apostel, writing for his colleagues in mathematics, describes eight ways in which models perform in his field. After a careful technical description of those functions, he summarizes them as "theory formation, simplification, reduction, extension, adequation, explanation, concretization, globalization, action or experimentation."[34] Kevin Clarke and David Primo itemize the functions of models in the social sciences:

> Theoretical models, we argue, can be useful in any one or more of four different roles: foundational (providing a basis for further model building or constructing a flexible and adaptive model), organizational (collecting disparate empirical generalizations, theoretical results, or set of facts under a single framework), exploratory (investigating mechanisms or motivations underlying phenomena of interest), and predictive (generating comparative statics). Empirical models are useful in one or more of three different roles: prediction (postdicting and forecasting), measurement (improving the quantification of difficult concepts), and characterization (describing data and spotting provocative associations). We argue that a fourth use of empirical models, theory testing, is the one for which they are least suited.[35]

These abstract analyses of models' functions contrast with the practicality of the assessment of business models' functions. Charles

Baden-Fuller, a business school professor, and Mary Morgan, an economic historian, offer an apology for models to the audience of business people. Corporate types, in contrast to quantitative scientists, apparently don't particularly value models. Baden-Fuller and Morgan describe how, in the business world, models function in three ways. Models act like scale models, as taxonomic descriptions of operations; they act like the model organisms in biology, as instruments of investigation; and they act like recipes, as practical models of procedures ready for copying or limited variation.[36] The function of models is even more pragmatically rendered in business manuals:[37]

> Managers use models in a variety of ways and for a variety of reasons. Models are beneficial because they 1. Are easy to use and less expensive than dealing with the actual situation. 2. Require users to organize and sometimes quantify information and, in the process, often indicate areas where additional information is needed. 3. Increase understanding of the problem. 4. Enable managers to analyze what-if questions. 5. Serve as a consistent tool for evaluation and provide a standardized format for analyzing a problem. 6. Enable users to bring the power of mathematics to bear on a problem.[38]

Although enumerations of models' functions may have practical applications, such lists of how they act can never be exhaustive. Not only are their specific functions as varied as their makers and consumers, but also, as autonomous agents, models often act in ways unintended by either. Because models always either exceed or resist the work assigned to them, any inventory the jobs that they do will inevitably be incomplete.

If a practical definition of all models must eschew listing their employments, it may nevertheless suggest something of their broader purpose. Although my sampling of the functions of models only gestures at the range of their occupations, it does indicate something about the ethics of their operations. I use "ethics" here to mean simply "the rules of conduct recognized in respect to a particular class of human actions or a particular group, culture, etc."[39] Models exhibit a certain standard of acceptable behavior in how they act, if not in what they are meant to accomplish. Central to an understanding of the ethics of models is their relation to the truth. As scientists have established, models are not "truth-apt." But the truthlessness of models does not mean that models are *necessarily* either liars or bullshitters. A lie is a false statement meant to deceive; liars know the truth but pervert it for their own benefit. Bullshitters, though also acting in their own interests, may not even know what truth is and they certainly don't care.[40] Of course there exist models that are liars and bullshitters. The economist Henry Ergas, for example, points to false models produced by the state as political propaganda. In his "Charter for Modelling Honesty," he specifies bad models as those that, for special interests, corrupt the data on which they are based and/or fail to disclose their data's sources. More familiar are bad models that elicit bad behaviors. A racist president is a model that provokes the worst in the people who elected him. A Barbie doll, which distorts the female body, might be understood as a bad model if it acts as a cue for bulimia. In contrast, good models do their best to help us get to the truth of the world. Good models relate to the truth like good mothers relate to perfect mothering: they strive to get there even though the goal is impossible. The ways in which models may work toward truth take a variety of forms. Models may be fictions, metaphors, or even caricatures.[41] But none of the various ways in which the work of models is characterized necessarily compromises a good model's objective to get closer to the truth of the world.

Good, respectable models work to make the world in some way or another more accessible. In the model-making process itself, in the action of modifying the model to get it to act more like its referent, or even in the deep engagement of critically thinking about a finished model, a good model offers a fuller understanding of the bit of the world that it models. That is, ethical models work as epistemic operators, as educators. It is commonly argued that making a model is more educational than simply contemplating the final product. Morgan and Morrison observe: "We do not learn much from looking at a model—we learn more from building the model and from manipulating it."[42] The urban planner Marcial Echenique also recognizes the importance of manipulation: "The main purpose of a model is to provide a simplified and intelligible picture of reality in order to understand it better. It should be possible to manipulate the model in order to propose improvements in [the model's representation of] reality."[43] Augmenting a climate change model with interactive atmospheric aerosols, atmospheric chemistries, and representations of the carbon cycle not only provides a more accurate image of the world, but also allows the modeler new insight into the world's processes.[44] In the arts and humanities too, making is usually more generative than looking. By sketching the Buddhas of Bamiyan or writing a book about models, the artist or author usually learns more about her object than does the viewer of the drawing or the reader of the book. Nevertheless, the active scrutiny of a finished model, the critical search for its weaknesses and strengths undertaken before accepting its interpretation of the world, is also a kind of manipulation that generates knowledge.

Toy models suggest something further about the way that all models work. The child playing with a doll's house adds furniture to it or rearranges its appurtenances to make it correspond more closely to lived or imagined conditions. In that process he better understands the domestic relations between objects and their possessors.[45] The doll's house, like other model toys, suggests that "play" is a productive way to understand models and their manipulation, at least if "play" is understood in terms of its definition by the Dutch historian Johan Huizinga.[46] In *Homo Ludens,* Huizinga argues that play is necessary, free, disinterested, reproducible, space- and rule-bound, potentially magical, and antifascist.[47] Some aspects of play articulated by Huizinga would seem usefully applicable not only to the manipulation of models, but also to models themselves: "Inside the play-ground [model space] an absolute and peculiar order reigns. Here we come across another, very positive feature of play [the model]: it creates order, is order. Into an imperfect world and into the confusion of life it brings a temporary, a limited perfection. Play [the model] demands order absolute and supreme.... Play [the model] casts a spell over us; it is 'enchanting,' 'captivating.'"[48]

The proposition that models are vehicles for investigating the world seems acceptable. Models provide a mechanism for probing the world's reality if not fully realizing its truth. It is, consequently, legitimate not only to make practical judgments about models (useful/not useful), but also ethical, if not moral, ones (good/bad). Through this discussion of models' operations, my definition might be further elaborated.

> A model is an autonomous agent that has a referent (material, ideal, conceptual, imaginary, . . .) to which it adverts (mimetically, symbolically, symptomatically, inferentially, . . .), but from which it differs in significant ways (in its complexity, scale, material, function, way of being-in-the-world, . . .). In its relation to its referent, a model is weak or strong and sometimes oscillating between the two. A model assumes its interpreter's familiarity with its particular hermeneutic conventions. Although no model can ever licitly make truth claims, a model can be *good or bad, honest or dishonest. A good model is an epistemic operator that works (abstractly, critically, ludically . . .) toward a fuller understanding of the world.*

This definition of model is based on common language and informed by the assessments made of models in the sciences and social sciences. I hope that it may prove of interest to artists and humanists in thinking about their models. For scientists and social scientists, the definition's description of models may be too familiar to be very helpful. The following two chapters consider two model types—bodies and buildings—from a humanist's perspective. The conclusions about model representation and model history drawn from those investigations may be novel enough to scientists and social scientists to be of some use to them.

2
Body Model/Science/History

> In examining the brain and its parts there is nothing to be gained by vivisection, since here, whether we like it or not, we are required by the theologians of our own day to deny that dumb animals have memory, reason or thought, even though the construction of their brain is the same as that of the human one.
>
> —Vesalius, *The Fabric of the Human Body,* mid-sixteenth century

THE CADAVER was essential to the emergence of one of the great scientific traditions in the West—medicine. It is a model with a history that is particularly rich and well documented both textually and visually. It is also a model to which every reader, not just the specialist, can relate: potentially, after all, every reader could become one. Most critically, the cadaver offers generative resistance to my definition of a model, both as it stands and as I want to extend it. A model must have a referent from which it is distinct. With the body model, the model and its human referent do not appear to be systemically different. The body model also appears ahistorical in so far as it is apparently unchanged: a cadaver in third-century BCE Alexandria, it might seem, was not significantly different from one in the Duke University Medical School gross anatomy lab today.

The first problem, the distinction between the body model and its human referent, is easily resolved. The term "model" is now commonly applied to bodies that work for artists, clothing designers, and Miss Universe contest organizers. Although the body of such a model belongs to a particular human, in its function as *model* that body is idealized, abstracted, and commoditized. The life of its possessor, though often enough discussed in popular media, hardly matters; her intellect is not of interest. All that counts is appearance. The model is presented as the paradigmatic way humans should look. The cadaver in a gross anatomy lab functions in much the same manner as a fashion model. Her life and intellect are not a concern. She also claims to be paradigmatic of the way humans should look, though that semblance lies primarily within the body rather than on its surface. She too is idealized and abstracted. She is distinct from the fashion model in that she resists commoditization.[1]

Both the cadaver and the supermodel differ from their referents—ordinary human beings whose bodies need to be accessorized or healed. A supermodel is distinct from her referents not only in her social context, her age, and her occupation, but also most crucially in her proportions and her flawlessness. Everything she wears looks good on her; the same cannot be said of her referents in the audience. In contrast, the best body model for medical schools is that which differs as little as possible from her referents. But just as fashion models (who generally act vertically) must meet certain height and weight requirements, cadavers (who generally act horizontally) must now conform to length and weight restrictions in order to be accepted into body donation programs. At least in the United States, bodies used for medical training are thereby increasingly distinguished from those in the general population: the obese are unacceptable.[2] But the body model differs from her referent even more dramatically than the fashion model does from hers: the body model is a dead human and her referents are live ones. The supermodel and the medical body model are not only distinct from their referent; they both also shift in the relative strength of their relationship to it. Édouard Manet's famous painting *Olympia* is a weak model of the artist's favorite sitter, Victorine Meurent, but it a strong model of modernist painting. Like Manet's painting, the medical body model oscillates between strength and weakness. The cadaver may be weak in relation to the ideal human body, but as a medical student's "first patient" or "silent teacher," she may be quite powerful in relation to those who later come under the doctor's care.[3]

That the medical body model is different from her referents is easily established. Identifying the ways in which a twenty-first-century cadaver is distinct from its earlier instantiations takes more work. My claim is that the body model is by no means stable: as society and technology change, so does the cadaver. Change is recorded in the cadaver's physical properties. Even more dramatically, cultural shifts are revealed in the cadaver's representations. How the body model is seen is, after all, disclosed by how it is depicted. Much has been written on the cadaver as a medical body model—the histories of its dissection, spectacularization, and abuse. Considerable research has also been published on the illustration of medical texts from antiquity to the present.[4] But I am not familiar with any extended consideration of how the dramatic shifts in representation from pre- to postmodernity in the West relate to changes to the cadaver's social and material being, to its essence. Here I offer a schematic sketch of parallel developments in the constitution of the medical body model and in its renderings. The two together reveal synergies in knowledge production.[5] As modifications in the materiality of the cadaver and in the modes of its representation are conditioned by cultural circumstances, medical body models offer useful documents of historical change. An assessment of premodern, early modern, modern, and contemporary Anthropocene examples both of cadavers and their images provides the basis for the first extension of my initial definition: *all models are historical.*

Index: Medieval Body Model

The beautifully illuminated medical miscellany of the late thirteenth century, Bodleian Library's Ashmole 399, is full of representations of the medical body model.[6] Its first full-page painting on folio 13v is a diagram of the reproductive system of a dissected human female (fig. 4). In the fundus of the uterus is the infant: a small, naked, but sexless human in an oval. The text framing the body identifies the subject: "Here the created seed has its place; here the infant is nourished and grows; here falls the semen and when it is fallen it is collected from the testicles."[7] Attached to the side of the uterus are those "testicles" (ovaries were commonly referred to as testicles in the Middle Ages and early modernity), neatly designated, as are all the other parts of the image. Almost all the elements on the left are marked "same here" as a mirror image of the features on the right. At the base of the uterus is the vaginal channel. The red borders are identified as ligaments (nerves); the teardrop shapes and gray strips are tagged

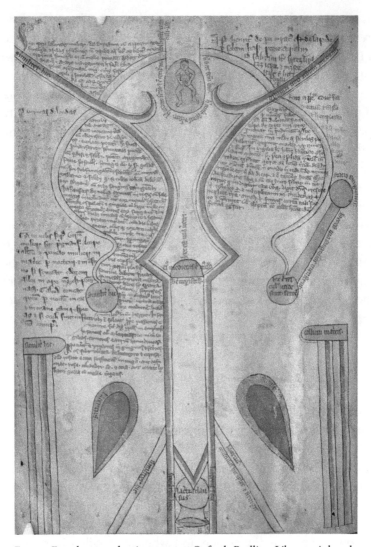

Fig. 4. Female reproductive system, Oxford, Bodlian Library, Ashmole 399, 1292 with later additions, 13v. (Bodleian Library)

as muscles. A comparison with a still from the twenty-first-century *Acland's Video Atlas of Human Anatomy* demonstrates that the image is a recognizable reading of its object (see fig. 9).[8] The medieval diagram depends on labels, while its Anthropocene counterpart depends on the running text of a voice-over. Both require verbal explanations.

The forms of the two representations express their respective cultural moments. The Ashmole image is unmistakably medieval. Its style is fully High Gothic: symmetrical, but not quite; curvilinear and calligraphic, but controlled. Its unmechanical, hand-drawn structures are elegantly architectural. The folio has the sensibility of the tracery of a contemporary church window.[9] The painting is a diagram of its object, rather than its visual impression. In ancient Greek, διάγραμμα is a line drawing or a sketch. Now, "diagram" commonly refers to a two-dimensional representation in which information about an object or concept is embedded. "Diagram" lurks in a liminal space between writing and drawing. A diagram, like all models, has a referent, but it stands in a consistently abstract relation with that referent.

The rendering of the female reproductive system on folio 13v of Ashmole 399 was not, of course, drawn by the illuminator from the direct observation of an anatomized body. Along with the other anatomical images in the work, its model was not a cadaver, but rather another, earlier manuscript illumination; it participates in a recension of images.[10] (The labeling of organs on the right, with their symmetrical counterparts on the left tagged simply as "same" perhaps suggests that the diagram originated in a right-to-left reading Arab society?) "Recension" is a specialized term used in philology to describe the family tree of premodern manuscripts. It has also been applied to premodern images.[11] This scholarly method attempts to establish the *original* form of a work, for instance, the New Testament. An urtext is reconstructed through the close comparative analysis of its various derivatives.[12] One of the assumptions of this method is devolutionary: copies are always inferior to the archetype because of the inevitability of scribal error. Recensions again attest to the oscillation of a model. A particular exemplar in a series, as a copy, offers a weak idea of the recension's archetype. At the same time, for the scribe who makes from it the next copy in the series, that same exemplar acts a strong model for a new generation of the recension. Before the printing press, each member of the recension was singular; each still retains the aura of an artwork. In contrast to mechanically reproduced images, whether printed or digitalized, history clings to the illumination—in the brushstrokes of its maker, in the flaws of its parchment platform, and, perhaps most important, in its unique imagistic and textual accretions. The notes that I make in my copy of *Gray's Anatomy* will never become part of that text's life in the way that scribal additions to Ashmole 399 have become part of its life.

In the fourteenth century, the diagram of the female reproductive system on folio 13v of Ashmole 399 was invaded by new texts.[13] The original emptiness of the composition may have contributed to the clarity of the diagram, but the spareness of its composition tempted a later scribe to fill in the interstices of its pattern. Those writings are recipes for improving women's health from Gilbertus Anglicus.[14] They do not *explain* the image of which they are a part, but they are relevant to its message, as are the essays both before and after it. Preceding the illumination is a copy of the *Liber de Physiognomia*, composed in the middle of the twelfth century; immediately following it is the *Tractatus obstetricius de forma uteri, et fetus in eo positionibus diversis; etiam de fetus formation* (*Obstetric treatise on the form of uteruses and on the different positions of the fetus; also on fetus formation*). Both of these works deal with the medical problems of human reproduction. In contrast to its labels, but like the writings that came to later inhabit the diagram, they complement the image rather than explain it. The scribes of both the contemporary and later texts evidently understood the diagram as they sought to amplify its meaning. Other texts in the miscellany are less obviously related to female anatomy. Alexander de Villa Dei's *Algorismus*, a treatise on the use of Arabic numbers, for example, has nothing at all to do with it.[15]

This illuminated diagram of a woman's reproductive system is not only enfolded in correlative texts, but also accompanied in the manuscript by other remarkable renderings: uteruses with fetuses, a diagram of the male genitalia, chiromantic drawings of the hands, five full-page illustrations of the body's systems (arteries, veins, bones, nerves, and muscles), and a quite wonderful diagram of the brain. There is also, in eight panels on four pages, a lively narrative illustration of the relationship between a wealthy female patient and her doctor.[16] That relationship ends badly with her dissection (fig. 5). This representation shows a familiarity with anatomization—the organs are enlarged, recognizably rendered, and carefully arranged on the picture plane for the

BODY MODEL/SCIENCE/HISTORY   29

FIG. 5. Dissection, Oxford, Bodlian Library, Ashmole 399, 34r. (Bodleian Library)

viewer's inspection. If the image suggests that dissection was known, it also implies that it was not socially acceptable. The anatomization occurs not in a building, but in the landscape. As in contemporary representations of Jesus's tormentors in the Passion, the anatomist is grotesque. He appears alarmed at being caught in the act. All of this is visual evidence that the procedure was at the time illicit, in contrast to the lawfulness of embalming or autopsy. It also implies that dissections did occur.

Although dissections are not attested in texts in England or northern France in the late Middle Ages, the narrative painting in Ashmole 399 suggests that they were carried out, even if clandestinely. The publication of a dissected thirteenth-century cadaver further supports such an assumption.[17] There are a variety of other references to medieval medical dissections. At one extreme, the heretic and felon Christianus was publicly vivisected by medical practitioners in Constantinople, perpetuating the tradition of vivisecting criminals attested in third-century BCE Alexandria.[18] The chronicler Theophanes (758–818) describes the occasion.

> Christianus, an apostate from the Christian faith and leader of the Scamari [armed brigands], was captured. They cut off his hands and feet on the mole of St. Thomas [in Constantinople], brought in physicians, and dissected him from his pubic region to his chest while he was alive. This they did with a view to understanding the structure of man. In this condition they gave him over to the flames.[19]

At the other extreme is the anatomizing of the saintly abbess Chiara di Montefalco, who died in 1308. Immediately after her death, her nuns embalmed her. They discovered signs of the Passion embedded in her viscera.[20] Chiara's anatomized heart subsequently performed miracles. The social location of the Western medieval medical body model was varied: it might have been abject, like that of the heretic Christianus, or holy, like that of the saintly Chiara. The few bodies that are attested were, whether despised or cherished, certainly identified and often familiar. Those cadavers were also fresh. People in the Middle Ages were much more familiar than we are with guts, mainly animal, but also human. The tortured and the wounded, heretics and saints, all revealed the workings of the body.[21]

Dissections were undertaken in the Middle Ages. The means of communicating what was found in these investigations was, however, limited to words and diagrams. When copies are made singularly and by hand, texts are easier to reproduce correctly than images, and simple, abstract forms are less subject to distortion than complex ones. Only a master miniaturist can reproduce images of great complexity, but scribes of varied skill levels can copy diagrams as well as texts with few errors. The mode of the image's production induced the simplification of its form, though certainly not its aesthetic persuasiveness or the complexity of its meaning. The work's abstraction was not, as some moderns might assume, representational incompetence.[22] Nor was it, as other moderns have posited, a matter of the remoteness from the body imposed by medievals' superstition, fear of contamination, and ignorance.[23] The diagram's artist, as well as its observers, may well have had some experience of the drawing's counterpart in nature—the uterus of a pig or a dog, if not a human. The diagrammatic abstraction of the female reproductive system is characteristic of many medieval representations of nonnarrative subjects such as architectural plans, cosmological orders, and maps.[24] The image is an *index:* the work effectively *points* to the significant aspects of its model by reducing it to a comprehensible system. Just as a book's index makes its subject matter accessible, so the diagram of this manuscript offers with remarkable conceptual clarity the "truth" of the body. In summary, the premodern medical image is an index of its cadaveric model, its diagram. The body that served as its referent was a familiar one, whether beloved like Chiara or despised like Christianus.

Icon: Early Modern Body Model

The Fabric of the Human Body, with a text by Andrea Vesalius and truly remarkable woodcuts ascribed to John Stephen of Calcar, an artist from Titian's workshop, appeared in 1543.[25] *The Fabric,* like Ashmole 399, produced two hundred and fifty years earlier, includes extraordinary images of both the female reproductive system and a narrative dissection of a woman.[26] The differences between the representations in the two works document the remarkable shifts that had occurred in early modern European technology and economy: most critically for our purposes, the invention of the printing press, the incorporation of woodcuts into print products, and the commercial success of the resulting publications. For the first time images could be cost-effectively rendered by highly trained artists, then reproduced with exactitude in hundreds of copies.[27] The possibility of making multiple facsimiles of detailed drawings stimulated those fields of human endeavor which depended for their development more on images (like anatomy and architecture) than on words and symbols (like theology and mathematics) or even diagrams (like geometry and astronomy). The production of high-quality, carefully observed representations of the body certainly proved a profitable investment for Vesalius. It also changed the way contemporaries thought about the body.[28]

The frontispiece of Vesalius's book, which has attracted intense scholarly attention, itself exquisitely represents attention (fig. 6).[29] The architecture stages an enclosed, elite space in which members of an all-male audience jostle indecorously to see the naked woman at its center. The carnivalesque character of the depiction is marked in the grotesques that inhabit it and the laughing skeleton which looks away from the woman but designates his attention to her with his staff. The table on which the body lies is tipped upward so that the reader is provided the best possible view of the vulnerable body. That body has been opened by the author, who looks at us at the same time that he, like the skeleton, shows his attention to the body by his gesture. He holds back a flap of skin, revealing the site of the cadaver's reproductive organs. The monkey and the dog in the lower corners of the print, who await their turn for dissection, suggest that the female object of the image is not fully human. Indeed, like the dog and the monkey, the woman is not a member of the same human community as her audience. She was an alien and a criminal, as well as being a woman. Although Vesalius certainly knew her name, he does not use it. He does, however, describe her physically and socially. She had an exceptionally large stature and had given birth many times. She was a woman condemned to death, who attempted to delay her execution by claiming that she was pregnant.[30] Law codes of sixteenth-century Italy further suggest that she was not native to the city in which she

BODY MODEL/SCIENCE/HISTORY   33

FIG. 6. Andreas Vesalius, *De humani corporis fabrica libri septem* (Basileae: Ex officina Joannis Oporini, 1543), frontispiece. (David M. Rubenstein Rare Book and Manuscript Library, Duke University)

was dissected: the only bodies *legally* provided anatomists were those of alien criminals.[31] Medical body models could not be members of the body politic; they had to be foreigners residing a specified distance beyond the borders of the state in which they were executed. One of Vesalius's better documented cadavers was Giacomo Bontadino, who murdered his own son. Not a citizen of Bologna, he was executed there on January 14, 1540.[32] He was immediately prepared for "public" anatomization by Vesalius, who had journeyed to Bologna on the occasion of the execution. Like the frontispiece scene of *The Fabric*, Giacomo's anatomization was spectacle; nonmedical students paid a twenty-scudi admission charge.[33]

Vesalius's text and John Stephen of Calcar's figures did not depend only on the bodies of executed foreigners. The demand for dissectible bodies in early modernity was greater than the supply of criminals. As is well documented, that market was satisfied primarily through theft. In his text, Vesalius flagrantly recounts the illicit appropriation of a body. He does so with remarkable callousness and contempt for public authority:[34]

> The students at Padua snatched from her grave . . . and brought in for public dissection the elegant mistress of a monk at the church of St. Anthony here. She had apparently died from strangulation of the womb or a stroke. With astonishing industry, they had removed all the skin from the cadaver so she would not be recognized by the monk, who with the prostitute's parents, was complaining to the urban prefect that the body had been stolen.[35]

The monk's mistress is literally stripped of her personhood in her preparation for dissection: again, she is not named in the text, and her anonymity is assured by the efficient flaying of her body by Vesalius's students. The burlesque treatment of the affair in Vesalius's book is rendered with equal insouciance in the volume's historiated initials.[36] The letter "I" depicts putti (cherubs) stealing a body in the middle of the night, as indicated by the torch.[37] The abject status of the cadaver in early modernity and modernity is revealed in its abuse, which is well documented.[38] The lack of propriety with which the body is treated is indicative of its loss of subjectivity. The human body is the abject object of male investigation, and so it remained through much of the twentieth century.

Despite the exaggerated emphasis on the female body in the narrative frontispiece of Vesalius's volume, the text that it introduces systematically investigates only the male body—beginning with the skeleton, then the muscles and gut, culminating in the head. The book's lavish full-page illustrations of that body in various stages of dissection are famous both for their verisimilitude and for the classical tropes that they enact. In the full-page, full-figure images of books 1 and 2, flayed bodies do not lie quietly but pose for their observers, fully participating in their own dissections by displaying their bones or their musculature like runway supermodels. The internal organs of book 5 are depicted in a series of male torsos that morph from those of handsome cadavers to those of classical statuary. The display of the male reproductive system is followed by that of the female. The representation of female anatomy is limited to two partial-page figures of her reproductive system and of the uterus and vagina removed from her body. No trace remains of the abjection of the criminal or stolen body from which these images, male or female, were made.

The rendering of the female reproductive system exposes a carefully described, veristic anatomy within the idealized marble encasement of a Hellenistic torso (fig. 7). Like the architecture of the dissection theater of the frontispiece, the display of organs within a classical frame elevates the subject and disguises the wretchedness of the real body that is the subject of the image and of the action. It was not only the classical iconography that elevated its status, but also its classical form. The artist depicted the human interior with that balance of clarity and naturalism, that idealized mimesis, associated with classical styles. The abject body of the criminal alien or of the socially marginal is persuasively masked by the visual rhetoric of the elite object. The rendering of the body model in Vesalius's *Fabric* may be characterized as that of a refined imitation of nature; it offers information about its subject not by diagraming it but by reproducing its idealized appearance. For the sake of clarity, I'll identify the early modern image as an *icon* of its cadaveric model, the cadaver's mimetic, idealized representation. But, however refined in its rendering, the medical body model in sixteenth-century Italy was an abject object, whether it was the legally acquired corpse of the criminal or the illicit, stolen cadaver of the vulnerable. The beautiful and complex visualizations of the human anatomy that

36   MODELS AND WORLD MAKING

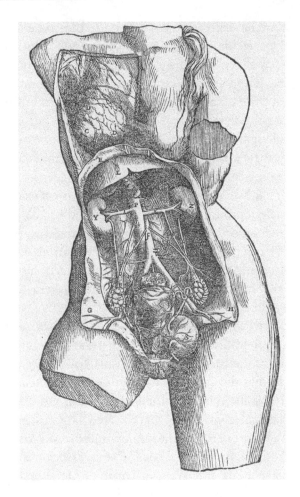

FIG. 7. Female reproductive system. Andreas Vesalius, *De humani corporis fabrica libri septem* (Basileae: Ex officina Joannis Oporini, 1543), 378. (David M. Rubenstein Rare Book and Manuscript Library, Duke University)

appear in Vesalius's text hint at those equally dramatic changes that occurred in the social and physical disposition of its medical body model, though primarily by disguising them.

Analog: Modern Body Model

The cadaver in the Middle Ages, whether beloved or despised, was rarely anonymous. In early modernity that changed. From the seventeenth century through most of the twentieth century in the global

North and on to the present in many parts of the world, the cadaver has been an anonymous, abject object. Early modern images mask the body model's abjection by beautifying it; modern images performed the same task through objectification. In modernity the cadaver, its representation, and its social location continued to be transformed, like the rest of society, by technology: the body model came to be treated as the quantitative analog of its human referent—its measurable equivalent.

"Analog" is a complex term; how it is used here in relation to images requires an explanation. In ancient Greek, αναλογία is proportion, ratio. Now, αναλογία's derivatives, "analog" and "analogy," act in a variety of related ways. Most commonly, "analogy" is simply a comparison of one thing to another in order to better understand it, as in William Paley's observation: "What is true of the other senses, is most probably true of the eye (the analogy is irresistible), viz. that there belongs to it an original constitution, fitted to receive pleasure from some impressions, and pain from others."[39] Paley also developed the more famous analogy between God and a watchmaker, which has been so fundamental to the argument for the existence of God on the basis of intelligent design. Paley's quote also demonstrates the use of analogy as a mode of argument. Charles Peirce explains: "Analogy is the inference that a not very large collection of objects which agree in various respects may very likely agree in another respect. For instance, the earth and Mars agree in so many respects that it seems not unlikely they may agree in being inhabited."[40] "Analog," as a noun, is the object in a comparison: for Paley, the watchmaker is the analog of God. In modernity, "analog" has been commonly used as an adjective to describe a device that imposes a numerical measurement on some aspect of experience (e.g., time or space). Such a device offers its users a numerical analogy to its referent, allowing some sense of control: a clock quantifies time: a map quantifies space. Now "analog" is deployed, willy-nilly, often independently of any object, in opposition to "digital."[41] Here, in relation to images, I deploy "analog" with its more traditional reference to quantified resemblance.

The impact of modern technology on the representation of the body model is demonstrated by plate 6 from William Hunter's *Gravid*

Uterus, drawn by Jan van Rymsdyk, engraved by Robert Strange in 1750, and published in 1774 (fig. 8).[42] The image is terrifying. Occupying a full page of an elephant folio, the full-scale, perfectly formed dead infant curls in an opened womb.[43] The brutality of the representation appalls: the dead mother's severed thighs and bisected vagina are graphically depicted. The horror of the picture is intensified by the contrast between the butchered body and its exquisite and hyperdetailed rendering.[44] The delicate modulations of the flesh are compelling; the figure's volumes are consistently defined not by an outline, which abstracts objects from nature, but by hatching, which imitates nature's shadowing. The reality of this representation remains, even in our own simulation-saturated twenty-first century, shocking. The

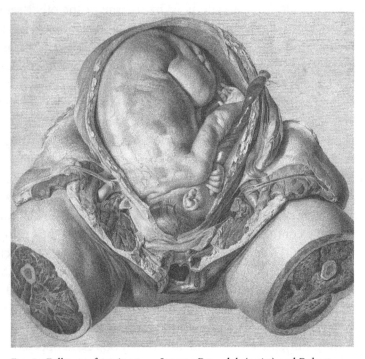

FIG. 8. Full-term fetus in utero. Jan van Rymsdyk (artist) and Robert Strange (engraver) in William Hunter, *Anatomia uteri humani gravidi tabulis illustrata* (Birmingham and London: S. Baker, T. Cadell, D. Wilson, T. Nichol, and J. Murray, 1774), pl. 6. (David M. Rubenstein Rare Book and Manuscript Library, Duke University)

interest in reproducing, on a two-dimensional surface, an impression similar to that made on the retina was not new, as Leonardo's 1511 realistic rendering of the dissected gravid uterus demonstrates.[45] Leonardo's drawings are fascinating and beautiful, not scary. Even Rymsdyk's original red-chalk drawing from which the etching was made, though realized on the same scale and with the same detail, is less alarming.[46] The warmth of the chalk's hue and its marks' caress of the paper both offer a trace of a human artist. That humanness is lost in the precision mechanics of engraving. The clinical clarity of the print contributes to its visual implacability.[47]

Engraved plates displaced woodcuts as the privileged technology of book illustration in the eighteenth century.[48] The technological process of engraving involves the incising of lines with a burin into a copper plate, the inking, wiping, and, finally, the impressing of the plate on paper. The ink in the incised lines is transferred to the dampened paper, creating a reverse image of the plate. The excavation of a line in metal is as slavish as a gesture in chalk is free. The engraver's task is one of consummate control; the reproduction of an artist's image requires the denial of his own expression. In the nineteenth century, engraved plates were superseded by lithographic stones as the favored medium of printed images. In lithography the printmaker applies the glue that holds the ink with a brush like a painter, whose skillset she shares. Lithographs lend themselves to the picturesque. In contrast, the power of Strange's engraving of Rymsdyk's drawing lies at least in part in its superb and calculated discipline.

The *Gravid Uterus* became one of the most prominent representations of the medical body model in modernity. The conditions of its production are symptomatic of the new social forces that emerged in the eighteenth century and became even more robust in the nineteenth and twentieth. The extension of European power stimulated exploration not only of remote parts of the world, but also of the recesses of the self and the self's immediate environment. New technologies, new elites, new institutions, and new appetites responded to new wealth and, at the same time, increased demand for accumulation. All of these factors were engaged in the making both the *Gravid Uterus* and its cadaveric model.

An elevated appetite for new knowledge and for high-quality artifacts associated with that new knowledge characterized the genesis of nonaristocratic connoisseurs. William Hunter, who commissioned the *Gravid Uterus* and who prepared its model, was himself one of the cognoscenti emerging as a cultural force in eighteenth-century England. Hunter was a distinguished physician trained in Glasgow, London, and Paris. He established a practice in London, where he specialized in obstetrics at a time when "male midwives," as such doctors were labeled, were still disdained by their medical colleagues. Despite being appointed physician extraordinary to the fecund Queen Charlotte, his field precluded his election to the Royal College of Physicians in London.[49] Hunter's remarkable intellectual as well as practical work in obstetrics ultimately contributed to the professional recognition of the specialization, the displacement of midwives by male doctors, and, more broadly, the medicalization of society.

Hunter's interest in women's bodies extended to bodies in general. He was identified as the man who established the study of anatomy as a serious discipline in England, after the butchers lost control of anatomizing.[50] He was such a prominent teacher of anatomy that, in 1768, he was appointed to the first chair of anatomy in the Royal Academy of Art. As in the print of the gravid uterus that he commissioned, Hunter insisted on hyperempiricism from his students. In his lectures he urged absolute attention to anatomical detail: "A painter or sculptor in executing a single figure in the ordinary situation of quiet life cannot copy Nature too exactly, or make deception too strong.... When a Painter finds that people who go into his room, bow to one picture, speak to another, and go into fits from the distraction of the situation, or when a statuary [sculptor] has but good information that young men have made serious attempts upon his Vestal, it will be time enough to say that the resemblance may be too perfect."[51] As models for his art students, Hunter famously used casts made of executed felons. His "Muscle Man" is depicted in a painting by Johann Zoffany that represents William Hunter lecturing in the Royal Academy.[52] Just as a painter objectifies his model by arranging her for his production, so Hunter posed his figures before *rigor mortis* occurred. "[As the work of procuring the body from the scaffold] was done in a few hours after death, and as [the cadaver] had not become stiff, Dr. Hunter conceived he might first be put into an attitude and allowed to stiffen in it, which was done, and when he became stiff we all set to work and by the next morning we had the external muscles all well exposed ready for making a mold from him, the cast of which is now in the Royal Academy."[53] Another écorché, made by Hunter from a smuggler hung for his crimes and arranged before *rigor mortis* to mimic the famous Roman sculpture of the dying gladiator, also remains at the Academy, where he is fondly named Smugglerius.[54] Here the medical body model and the artist's model bleed uncannily into one another. These models are also uncomfortable in their reminiscence of Vesalius's figures and their prescience of Gunther von Hagens' *Body Worlds*. The study of anatomy was essential to artists' training in the eighteenth and nineteenth centuries. Less recognized was the importance of art to anatomists. In an 1827 advertisement for the medical course in anatomy that he offered, John Farre stipulated: "It is indeed highly desirable that all persons, who cultivate Medicine from a love of the science, should study painting, as far as it is subsidiary to the primary pursuit, for an accurate Sketch is a permanent Memorandum. He intends that every Student of the Academy, over whom he may have control or influence, shall both Dissect and Sketch."[55]

William Hunter was an innovator in the preparation of cadaveric models as well as in their reproduction.[56] An American doctor, John Morgan, described a process by which veins and arteries might be studied by injecting them with a colored wax solution. He notes that "the first rudiments of this art that I acquired was from the two Hunters [William and his brother John]."[57] William was particularly well known for his improvements in embalming techniques. One peculiar example described by a fellow doctor, John Knyveton, demonstrates the performative capacities of embalming:

> Calling one day last month at Dr. William Hunter's, found William Cruikshank [Hunter's assistant] busily engaged embalming the body of a female by injecting her veins with oil of turpentine and camphorated spirit of wine, and packing camphor into the abdomen: and learnt she was the late wife of Mr. Martin van Burchell [*sic*], a white-bearded

old hypocrite of a self-styled Dentist, residing at Mount Street, Mayfair: who rides in the Row on fine mornings armed with a large bone and riding a spotted pony. As Mr. Cruikshank was successful in injecting a carmine liquid into the body, giving it a life-like color, and glass eyes of the natural color were inserted, the deceased finally presented quite a lively appearance: and now Mr. Burchell, having arrayed his spouse in a linen gown and lace, and put her in a glass case behind a curtain in his office, exhibits his 'dear departed,' as he styles her, to the public "Any day between the hours of Nine and One except Sunday's."[58]

Hunter dissected his models and prepared his specimens in a mixed-use building on Great Windmill Street near Piccadilly Circus, which he planned in collaboration with the Scottish architect Robert Mylne.[59] The structure housed not only Hunter's dissection preparation room and a laboratory for specimen production, but also his residence, a garden, a stable, and a yard for burying human remains. It also incorporated teaching spaces for Hunter's school of medicine. Hunter lectured on gross anatomy with dissected cadavers. To facilitate the inspection of smaller body parts, he circulated specimens, many of which he had harvested himself. To keep the samples intact, Hunter directed students to look at them closely, but not to manipulate them for fear of damage. The centrality of the specimen to Hunter's educational project is suggested by his admonition to his pupils: "I must earnestly recommend it to every student to make and collect as many anatomical preparations as he can."[60] To do so required, of course, a familiarity with dissection.[61] Demonstrations took place in a specially designed lecture hall, which Hunter describes:

> You may observe that this theatre is particularly well constructed, both for seeing and hearing; a strong sky-light is thrown upon the table, and the glass being ground, that is, made rough upon one surface, the glare of sun-shine is not admitted: the circular seats are brought as near the table, as ease in fitting would admit of; and, as they go back, they are a good deal raised, which is considerable advantage both in seeing and hearing; you may observe another circumstance in this theatre, which has not been sufficiently considered in buildings

of that kind, viz. the table, where the object is placed, and by which the demonstrator stands, is not in the center of the circular room, but about half way between the center and the circumference; thence the seats make smaller segments of larger circles, in proportion as they are farther removed; and the spectators, in proportion as they are at a greater distance, are more directly before the object and speaker, which, both in hearing and seeing, makes some compensation for the greater distance.[62]

Hunter's emphasis on architectural design in the service of seeing and hearing demonstrates his desire to convey with clarity the newly discovered truths of science.

A second large, semipublic space in the Great Windmill Street complex served the same purpose in a different way: display. Anatomical specimens had, in the eighteenth and nineteenth centuries, an acknowledged educational mission.

> It must be admitted that a collection in which all the organs would be disposed in series, where they would be seen passing by their successive degrees of increment and decrement, offering their differences, individual and sexual, their points of contact and separation in the various classes of the animal kingdom, their anomalies, their pathological affections, their intimate structure, &c., it must be admitted I say, that such a collection would be an inexhaustible source of knowledge; it would acquire additional value by the addition of a series of pieces representing the detailed anatomy of each of the parts involved in surgical operations.[63]

Hunter aspired to offer such a collection to a limited, educated, elite public. The Danish entomologist Johann Fabricius described the space of display in 1784:[64]

> The cabinet consists of a great and high room, covered by a dome through which the light falls. . . . At mid-elevation circling the entire room is a low gallery, and here is arranged the best collection, perhaps in Europe, of anatomical preparations, some dry, some in alcohol. . . .

The beautiful large illustrations of the uterus that Dr. Hunter published some years ago were engraved based on these specimens.[65]

The exhibition space offered more than an education in human anatomy. It presented a systematic treatment of other aspects of the natural and social world. Hunter's last will and testament gives a sense of the breadth of his acquisitive interests:

> I give and bequeath all and singular my Books printed and Manuscript, Prints and Books of Prints, engraved Copper-plates, Drawings, Pictures, Medals and Coins, Anatomical Preparations of every kind, Fossils and Ores, Shells, Corals, and other marine productions, Birds, Insects and all other preserved animals or parts of Animals, dried Plants, Curiosities from the South Seas, and whatever can be naturally reckoned a part of my Collection of Curiosities, all the cabinets cases and apparatus for containing and preserving these above article, Instruments for anatomy & surgery, and a chased silver cup which was presented to me by the students of anatomy.[66]

His "Curiosities from the South Seas" came from Captain James Cook's explorations.[67] Fabricius, the entomologist, noted that Hunter's collection of insects was the best in London.[68] Eclectic collecting was hardly novel, but Hunter's understanding of their exhibition was new. Fabricius identified Hunter's display space as a "cabinet," and Hunter himself named his precious things "curiosities." Cabinets of curiosities were popular in the sixteenth and seventeenth centuries.[69] But the cabinet was typically a private space, and a curiosity is a thing that appeals because of its oddity. Hunter's objects were disciplined by their order and controlled by their labels so that they might function as knowledge of the world. Hunter identified this space not as a cabinet, but as a museum. In the eighteenth century, the museum was still a newish institution; it had not yet matured into the segregated site that it became in the nineteenth and twentieth centuries, in which crafts and medical specimens could not use the same bathrooms as the fine arts. Hunter's museum reveals modernity's new desire for science and appetite for the objects that that science engaged.[70] Appearing in the company of casts and wet specimens derived from the same cadaver, the extravagantly scaled and executed print of the gravid uterus represented the ultimate modern control of knowledge.[71] It was commissioned by Hunter to be of a quality worthy of exhibition in his own collection.[72] Jan van Rymsdyk/Robert Strange's print of the *Gravid Uterus* would still now feel more at home in a modern art museum then in a science one.

All museums involve violence.[73] Hunter's assembly of human body parts and their representations is a particularly literal expression of the necessity of destruction for the sake of mastery, preservation, collection, and display. Hunter's medical exhibition—its prints as well as its casts and specimens—was made possible only by the many cadavers that supplied it. In England in the eighteenth century the only legally sanctioned dissectible body remained that of the executed felon. Modernity's ever-increasing demand for bodies was still largely met with stolen ones. Students and others pursuing anatomical research were commonly responsible for procuring their own bodies. Theft was still conventionally limited to the socially marginal, like Vesalius's monk's mistress. In the United States, the graveyards of African Americans were ravaged by medical students.[74] John Knyveton as a student doctor disinterred poor patients who had died under his care.[75] By the nineteenth century, the demand was so pressing that the bodies of those with social standing came under threat: the need for cadavers finally infringed on the sensibilities of the middle classes. Riots resulted. In 1824, for example, after the theft of the nineteen-year-old daughter of a substantial farmer from her grave in West Haven, Connecticut, local militia had to protect the Yale College of Medicine from being burned down by an angry mob.[76] There were even greater scandals when bodies for dissection were produced unnaturally, as in the case of William Burke's trial and execution in 1829 for the murder of sixteen men and women whose bodies had been sold to Dr. Robert Knox for anatomical demonstrations.[77]

New urban institutions emerged as an alternative source of cadavers in the eighteenth century. Charitable hospitals began to be founded in London in the later seventeenth century; their occupancy and prominence expanded the eighteenth.[78] Hunter had close ties to these foundations, most notably St. George's Hospital. In 1747 this charity foundation had 5,436 "objects under care."[79] Some of the bodies unclaimed at the time of their deaths no doubt appeared on Hunter's dissecting table. He thanks his colleagues for their help in providing for his work on the gravid uterus an unusually high number of female patients who, with their infants, died in labor. The names and sources of these patients remain unidentified in his text. Cadavers of pregnant women were difficult to obtain; Hunter's acquisition of over a dozen female cadavers in different states of pregnancy has even elicited the charge of murder.[80]

William Hunter was an early, unsuccessful advocate of the legalization of the use of unclaimed bodies as medical body models. In a petition submitted to the Earl of Bute, first Lord of the Treasury, Hunter opines:

> Scarce any science or art requires the protection of a prince more than Anatomy, as well on account of its great use to mankind, as because it is persecuted by the prejudices, both natural and religious, of the multitude in all nations. . . . The difficulties, dangers, and expenses, that must be incurred, in procuring dead bodies, and in providing proper places for dissection, and the secrecy with which the business must be conducted, are such discouragements to the study of Anatomy, that few men, even of the profession, ever attempt the practical part: and, without practice, there can be no great share of real and useful knowledge. . . . [England will lose its status as a center of anatomical science; the training of experts is impossible because] there is no provision made by our government for supplying him with subjects.[81]

Hunter failed in his efforts to have the appropriation of unclaimed bodies sanctioned by the state. His exploitation of bodies from charity institutions was certainly extralegal.[82]

In contrast to Vesalius, Hunter does not boast publicly of his students' prowess in obtaining bodies. On the contrary, he cautions students to be circumspect in their discussion of dissection outside the school.

> In a country where liberty disposes the people to licentiousness and outrage, and where Anatomists are not legally supplied with dead

bodies, particular care should be taken, to avoid given [*sic*] offence to the populace, or to the prejudices of our neighbors. Therefore it is to be hoped, that you will be upon your guard; and, out of doors, speak with caution of what may be passing here especially with respect to dead bodies.[83]

Hunter was also aware of the delicate issue of men looking at women's exposed bodies. Friends of students were allowed to attend anatomy lectures after they were properly introduced. "The lectures, however, upon the organs of generation, and gravid uterus, are to be excepted. No visitor can be introduced when we are upon these subjects. The reasons for such exceptions must be obvious."[84] While the process of looking at a female corpse and cutting into it might, for Hunter, be private, its representation was certainly public. Characteristic of the eighteenth century's modernity is Hunter's commodification in his *Gravid Uterus* of the brutal as the beautiful.

Growing outrage over the theft of bodies finally led to the legalization of the use of unclaimed bodies for anatomizing both in England and some states in the United States. The Anatomy Act, passed in Parliament in 1832, replaced the felon with the pauper.[85] With the rise of industrial capitalism, the bodies of the poor were outside society as they had not been in the Middle Ages. They were found to be as much of a burden to society in death as they had been in life. The medical profession relieved the community of its funerary obligations to noxious things.[86] The threat of dissection, which had been used as a deterrent for murder, was, after 1832, deployed as a deterrent to destitution.[87] The modern investigation of the body entailed the multiplication of abject body models. The body's scientific study, as Hunter's *Gravid Uterus* demonstrates, depended on its precise measurement, its systematic cataloging, and its analytical display. The modern body model, the abject cadaver, was its living referent's analogical equivalent.

Simulacrum: Anthropocene Body Model

The medical body model continues to change. The cadaver in the Anthropocene present is, in its social and material being, distinct from that of the modern. Lucy documents the difference. Lucy was one of forty cadavers in the anatomy lab in the basement of Duke Hospital in the fall of 2018, the object of study of five first-year medical students and myself. She was, to us, anonymous. Our team named her in order to avoid referencing the body as "it." Shortly after her death, Lucy was embalmed and refrigerated. Although she was as complex and idiosyncratic as her patient referents, she had lost her natural color and viscosity. She was heart-renderingly, humanly, present in the anatomy lab, but she was no longer "fresh," as were most earlier medical body models. She was also much less dangerous to her observers than were the toxic bodies of the recently dead used into the nineteenth century. In 1774, John Knyveton recorded the early death of a brilliant, thirty-five-year-old researcher from a fever brought on by a "dissection wound."[88] The distinguished French pharmacologist Jean-Nicolas Gannnal commented on the perils of dissection in his 1838 book on embalming: "But the corpse always exhales mephitic miasmata before all the organs are putrefied, and this emanation of gas is certainly the cause which most frequently determines typhus fever, so destructive to a portion of our studious youths." He adds in a note, "Out of ten medical students lodging together, and frequently of the same amphitheater, nine were attacked by this grave malady in the course of last year, and three of them died."[89] Embalming procedures, crude at the time of William Hunter, developed rapidly in the next century, particularly during the U.S. Civil War. Embalming allowed some semblance of a slaughtered soldier to be returned to his family. The same new technologies were applied to medical body models.[90] All of us working with Lucy survived our encounter with her.

The materiality of the body model, then, is significantly modified. So is her subjectivity. In further contrast to the body models of the past, who were either known or not known, Lucy was both. Beyond her age and cause of death, Lucy was to us anonymous. At the same time, she was well known by the administrator of the body donation program of the Duke University Medical School, who knew her or at least members of her family and who kept careful track of Lucy once she was in her care. Lucy preserved her personal history and indeed added to it. Like the anatomized saints of the Middle Ages, Lucy retained her aura.

She was and remains an integral part of her community, beloved and honored. The donated body, at every stage of her contribution, was carefully treated.[91] We were mentored on how we should appropriately behave with her.[92] After she made her final contribution to science, her dissected remains were cremated, then returned to her family or distributed in Duke Forest. Memorial services have been held in her honor, in which those of us who she educated expressed our gratitude to her.[93] The contemporary medical body model, at least in Europe and North America, may be understood, not as in the Middle Ages as a beloved subject, but as a beloved object. And not as in early modernity as an abject object, but as a cherished object.

A bizarre but symptomatic example of the emergence of this modified body model is offered by Jeremy Bentham (1748-1832), the well-known Utilitarian philosopher. Bentham was committed to providing science with the bodies needed for its advancement. He worked for the institution of the British Anatomy Act before he died. He arranged for his own body to be dissected immediately after his death. The intention of his donation is made clear in a document associated with his will:

> The manner in which Mr. Bentham's body is to be disposed of after his death The Head is to be prepared according to the specimen which Mr. Bentham has seen and approved of The Body is to be used as the means of illustrating a series of lectures to which scientific & literary men are to be invited These lectures are to expound the situation structure & functions of the different organs the arrangement & distribution of vessels & whatever may illustrate the mechanism by which the actions of the animal economy—are performed the object of these lectures being two fold first to communicate curious interesting & highly important knowledge & secondly to show that the primitive horror at dissection originates in ignorance & is kept up by misconception and that the human body when dissected instead of being an object of disgust is as much more beautiful than any other piece of mechanism as it is more curious and wonderful After such lectures have been given those organs which are capable of being preserved for example the heart the kidney &c &c to be prepared in whatever manner may be conceived to render their preservation the

most perfect and durable And finally when all the soft parts have been disposed of the bones are to be formed into a skeleton which after the head prepared in the manner already stated has been attached to it is to be dressed in the clothes usually worn by Mr. Bentham & in this manner to be perpetually preserved. April 13 1830.[94]

In this act, Bentham exemplifies a truly dramatic shift in the medical body model: it is given rather than taken. Care is accorded to a donated body of a sort not extended to an abject object. The donated body is both a privileged body and a preserved one. Bentham exerted control over his body after he was dead: it was dissected then reconstructed, encased, and housed in the college that he established. He still travels.[95] Lucy also determined the disposition of her remains, though in a different way. Both are cherished objects.

Bentham's body donation remained anomalous until the late twentieth century. Now, in some institutions, like Duke University, only donated bodies are used for the educational purposes of dissection.[96] The public embrace of the donation of the body for the benefit of medical science was preceded and enabled by the broad acceptance of cremation.[97] Adoption of cremation as an appropriate way to treat the beloved body depended on changed cultural and religious prejudices.[98] The expansion of the middle class and the attendant modifications in the social assumptions of Protestantized societies of Europe and North America contributed to the loss of unclaimed bodies to anatomy labs in those regions. With the broad reforms of the later nineteenth and early twentieth century (child labor laws, universal education, voting enfranchisement), the appropriation of the poor body for anatomization came under increasingly incensed moral scrutiny.[99] The secularization of society also brought about a secularization of the body. Protestants gave up harvesting relics from famous preachers, like George Whitefield; locks of hair were no longer given to relatives and friends at the deathbed.[100] As body parts lost their aura, so did the body as a whole. Inhumation, the burial of the intact body, had been standard practice in the West since the Christian suppression of traditional Greco-Roman religions. Burning bodies, even those of heretics, was avoided in the Middle Ages.[101] So long as ways of disposing of bodies other than inhumation were anathema, anatomizing the corpse of a cherished family member remained unbearable. The emergence of cremation as socially acceptable changed that. Cremation, against the law in many countries in the West, became a cause for reformers in the 1870s.[102] It was legalized in England and many states in the United States in the early twentieth century.[103] It is worth noting that the Catholic church opposed cremation until 1963; cremation is still abhorred by Conservative and Orthodox Jews. Israel did not have a crematorium until 2003; ultra-Orthodox arsonists burned it down in 2007.[104] Nevertheless, the popularization of cremation as an appropriate way of treating the beloved body is symptomatic of modernity's secular adaptation to economic and technological change.

The change in the representation of the medical body model in the Anthropocene is even more dramatic than the modifications in her physical and social constitution. The dominant contemporary image of the medical body model is hyperreal.[105] There are many technologies by which such images are produced—from the Visible Human Project's MRI scans of cadaver slices to the plastinated bodies of Gunther von Hagen's notorious Body World Exhibitions—all of which share some features of their production, consumption, and commoditization.[106] One of those modes of representation is *Acland's Video Atlas of Human Anatomy*, which was used in our lab (fig. 9).[107] Here the digitalized dissection is presented as compellingly three-dimensional on our flat screens. In it, the female reproductive system is initially isolated, then rendered in place in a cadaver that was much fresher than Lucy. Acland's videos deploy a combination of conventional photographic and dissection techniques with new digital media to make the human interior present to its audience. Although not as "cutting edge" as the Visible Human Project, it perfectly describes our current culture's representational desires. The diagram of the Middle Ages, the icon of early modernity, and the analog of modernity have been displaced by a hyperreal, ectypic image, a simulacrum.[108] I use "simulacrum" broadly to refer to a dangerously credible appearance or representation of the untrue and nonexistent.[109]

The question now is whether the simulacrum will, as is its wont, replace the physical body model. Will Lucy be superseded by her

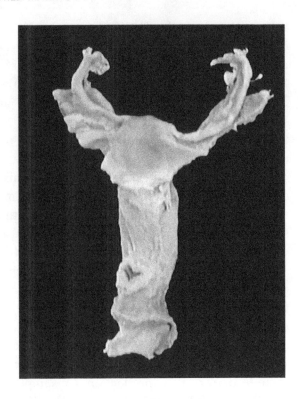

FIG. 9. Female reproductive system. *Acland's Video Atlas of Human Anatomy*, vol. 5, sec. 3 (https://aclandanatomy.com/, Wolters Kluwer Health, 2021). (Screen capture by the author)

representations in future anatomy labs?[110] In many of those places where the expense of body donation programs or regional cultural practices make it difficult to attain cadavers, they already have. Elaborate synthetic bodies and animated mannequins programed with various physical disabilities have been patented.[111] These objects have, however, so far, proven *very* weak models of the human body.[112] Computational representations do not as yet provide a full experience of the human body—its complex layering, its particular anomalies, its resistance to probing.[113] Lucy was scanned in preparation for her dissection. But my team consistently considered the body before it consulted the scan. The scan was always a weak copy. Like attempts to move the human on to a computational platform (a robot), efforts to replace cadavers with digital proxies have so far failed. A corpse is expensive to acquire and to maintain. Institutions make large capital investments in body donation programs, cadaver preparation, and dissection facilities; students endure formaldehyde and refrigeration. Despite their costs and liabilities, science, it seems, still needs bodies.[114] That need may come in for closer scrutiny after the widespread experience of online anatomy labs during the COVID-19 pandemic.

Cadavers and their representations participated fully in the unfolding of medical discourse. The body model and its images are not merely entangled in that discourse, but have been active agents in determining its development. The desire for understanding the body was aroused by what was seen or not seen in its representations. The need to represent ever more accurately the structure of the human interior stimulated refinements in both dissection techniques and in the preservation of the body. With the privatization and professionalization of anatomizing in the eighteenth and nineteenth century, the image assumed the burden of satisfying the desire of the broader public to witness their own interiors.[115] The broad cultural urge for increasingly veristic representation of the human anatomy was dialectically related to a new voyeurism of the self.

The contemporary cadaver is very different from that of third-century BCE Alexandria. Her social location is modified—she is a subject as well as an object. And her physical constitution is changed—she is safe, not dangerous. The preservative processes by which the corpse is sustained for the purposes of study have become much more effective. The cadaver's standing in the human community shifted from abject object to privileged subject. Modifications in the medical body model correspond to transformations in the way it was interpreted. Images of the body model conform to the visual habitus of their moment. The persuasiveness of the illuminations of Ashmole 399 depended on the affordances of manuscript making; the credibility of the images in the publications of Vesalius and Hunter was conditioned by the evolution of printing and printed illustrations; the authority of *Acland's Video Atlas* would not be possible without digitalization. More essentially, different historical modes of representation also embody different ways of seeing and understanding the world—diagrammatically, iconically, analogically, ectypically. The medical body model, like all models, is committedly historical.

3
Building Model/Architecture/Politics

> The IDF [Israel Defense Forces] has recently completed the production of 3-D computer models of the entire West Bank and Gaza, which provide intricate detail of individual houses, including the location of internal doors and windows.
>
> —Eyal Weizman, *Hollow Land*

NOT ONLY do all models have a history, they also all have a politics. The cadaver, the medical body model, is an unexpected site for exploring history; similarly, the architectural model is not initially an obvious object through which to probe politics.[1] After all, aren't model buildings about poetics, not politics?[2] What could possibly be political about a Lego model?[3] But even apparently innocent structures are always less than innocent; models are at least as manipulating as their referents. The premodern to Anthropocene sequence of models presented here reveals dramatic shifts in the conception, construction, and function of architectural models. Many changes recorded in architectural models are analogous to those identified in the representations of the medical body model, nuancing an understanding of the character and implications of historical shifts. The transformations of architectural models certainly reinforce the recognition of models as historical markers. More critically they reveal the remarkably consistent political force of models. They suggest that while some models may be subtle, micropolitical agents, others are aggressive, even dangerous, macropolitical ones.

To establish a historical paradigm, I have taken all my referents for the architectural models in this chapter from one city, Jerusalem. Jerusalem is a city of uncommon violence; its politics tend to the diabolical. Never at the core of a great empire, but often occupying a strategically important periphery, it has been subject to external aggression

BUILDING MODEL/ARCHITECTURE/POLITICS   55

from antiquity to the present. Internal dissension is also endemic in Jerusalem. The city was the great incubator of monotheisms with their attendant fanaticisms; religion continues to exacerbate urban brutality. In the present, the architecture and topography of Jerusalem fully participate in the city's violence, as demonstrated both by the Al-Aksa intifada, which was instigated on the site of the Dome of the Rock, and, more permanently, by the Israeli West Bank barrier wall. The built landscape of Jerusalem has, through the centuries, consistently contributed to its discord.

A central actor in the violent politics of Jerusalem is the Church of the Holy Sepulchre.[4] The Holy Sepulchre is a site of unrivaled sacredness for traditional Christian communities—Roman Catholics, Greek Orthodox, Armenians, Copts—who sporadically brawl over the possession of its spaces.[5] The Holy Sepulchre acted as a strong model of its many representations in premodern and early modern Europe. Those representations, though weak models of their powerful archetype, commonly exerted remarkable force on their environments by their absorption not only of their prototype's aura, but also its politics. The Holy Sepulchre, built in the fourth century CE by Constantine, the first Christian emperor, had from the beginning political as well as religious purposes. The complex included a basilica for the celebration of the liturgy, the bishop's residence, and a great rotunda sheltering the rock-cut tomb identified as that of Jesus. Its construction represented the triumphs of Christianity over Jews and pagans and of Constantine over his rival emperor, Licinius. The Islamic conquest of Jerusalem in the seventh century ended Christian hegemony in the city. The construction of Dome of the Rock on the site of Herod's Temple (destroyed by the Romans in 70 CE) ended the Holy Sepulchre's architectural dominance of the cityscape. Fires, destructions, decay, and partial reconstructions of the complex by both the Byzantines in the eleventh century and the Crusaders in the twelfth transformed the neatly ordered, late Roman complex into a medieval muddle (figs. 10 and 11).[6] Within this disorder, the site's most important ancient features remained legible: the great rotunda sheltering the aedicule of the empty, rock-cut tomb of Jesus and a liturgical space to the East for the celebration of the Eucharist. This spatial mess was the referent

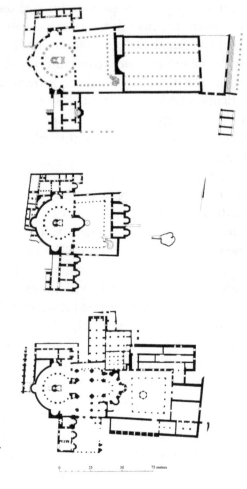

FIG. 10. Jerusalem, Church of the Holy Sepulchre. Top, 4th century; middle, 11th century; bottom, 12th century. (Sketch plans modified by the author from Robert Osterhout, "Architecture as Relic and the Construction of Sanctity: The Stones of the Holy Sepulchre," *Journal of the Society of Architectural Historians* 62 [2003]: 7–9)

for models that offered the most revered site in Christianity to pious Catholic audiences in the West.

Index: Medieval Building Model

The Temple Church, built in London on the north bank of the Thames not far from St. Paul's Cathedral during the First Crusade, is a model of the Holy Sepulchre (figs. 12 and 13).[7] The Temple Church's relation

FIG. 11. Jerusalem, Church of the Holy Sepulchre, south facade and main entrance, early twentieth-century photograph, American Colony (Jerusalem), Photo Department. (Library of Congress, Prints and Photographs Division, G. Eric and Edith Matson Photography Collection, LC-DIG-matpc-00019)

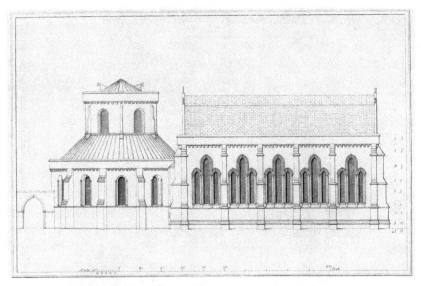

FIG. 12. London, Temple Church, south elevation. (Robert William Billings and Edward Clarkson, *Architectural Illustrations and Account of the Temple Church, London* [London: T. & W. Boone, 1838], pl. 3)

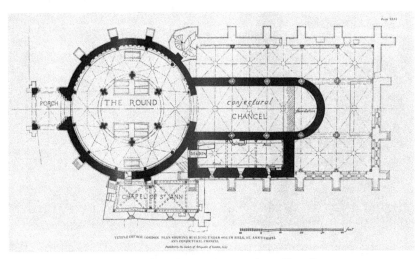

FIG. 13. London, Temple Church, plan. (Walter Hinds Godfrey, "Recent Discoveries at the Temple, London, and Notes on the Topography of the Site," *Archaeologia: Miscellaneous Tracts Relating to Antiquity* 95 [1953]: 123–40, pl. 46)

to its archetype is not, however, established through resemblance—it does not *look like* the Holy Sepulchre (compare fig. 11 and fig. 12). In modernity, we tend to think of "models of," especially models of buildings, as scale models, reproducing the forms, proportions, and appearances of their archetypes.[8] "Architectural portraits" of the scale model sort occasionally appear in the Middle Ages, most commonly in depictions of a building's donor presenting the structure as a gift to an emissary of the divine. For example, in the narthex of Hagia Sophia in Constantinople, a famous tenth-century mosaic depicts Constantine and Justinian offering respectively Constantinople and Hagia Sophia to the Virgin enthroned between them. However, without labels or context most medieval models of this sort are hard to identify with certainty.[9] They represented a particular building not so much by reproducing its appearance, but by abstractly referencing it: they were architectural emojis. The Temple Church was not a scale model of its archetype: its proportions and the articulation of its exterior bear no resemblance to the Holy Sepulchre. But it is much more than an emoji. It is an indexical model of its venerable archetype. The building effectively points to the significant aspects of its referent by reproducing its most prominent features. To paraphrase the simile given in chapter 2 describing folio 13v of Ashmole 399: just as a book's index makes its subject matter accessible, so the arrangement of volumes of the Temple Church offers with remarkable conceptual clarity the "truth" of its referent in Jerusalem.

The Temple Church has an obviously unusual configuration.[10] At its west end is "the Round," a twelfth-century rotunda. To the east extends a thirteenth-century, three-aisled basilica which replaced an earlier, single-aisled nave.[11] The Round controls the attention of the observer by its rotundity and monumentality. Circular buildings are not so common in the West; round churches—in which the conventional Western eucharistic liturgy fits rather badly—are relatively rare. The distinct figuration of the west end of the Temple Church not only attracts notice, but also elicits its reading as special. In the Middle Ages, the Round acted indexically, pointing to the Rotunda of the Holy Sepulchre. Like the Holy Sepulchre, though much more legibly, the Temple Church juxtaposes a rotunda with an oblong extension. The interior of the Temple Church, like its exterior, looks nothing like its archetype. Its volumes have a lightness, clarity, and coherence that contrast with the obscurity and incoherence of the Holy Sepulchre. The inside of the Temple makes the separation between the nave and the rotunda just as clear as does its outside.

The interior of the Temple Church also reveals what is masked externally: the space has competing focal points. The visceral presence of the Round with its dramatic vertical axis demands the congregant's attention be directed west. The altar, the locus of the sanctuary's officiating priest and its most important relics, insists that the congregant's attention be directed east. Western churches are conventionally controlled by a horizontal axis generated by the altar; if there is a vertical axis at the crossing it is secondary, marking the climax of the procession to the altar (Old St. Peter's in Rome) or at least its progress in that direction (Cathedral of Santiago de Compostela). The spatial hierarchy is unequivocal; the church is dominated by its high altar. In contrast, spatial order is ambivalent in the Temple Church. The attention of the congregant is split: the rotunda in the west contends with the altar in the east for the concentration of the pious beholder. When congregants participate in the Eucharist, they must turn their backs on the most compelling space of the building.

The Crusaders' remodeled Holy Sepulchre in Jerusalem, dedicated in 1149, created the same dilemma: the congregant's attention is divided between the altar to the east and the rotunda to the west.[12] There, the source of the western rotunda's vertical axis is clear—the tomb aedicule. What originally generated the central focus of the Round in London and its dramatic vertical axis is unknown because of the building's many restorations.[13] The knights' funerary effigies now occupying the central space were relocated there in the nineteenth century. Perhaps, like its archetype, a (portable?) tomb aedicule occupied its center. Or perhaps the Temple's two poles were liturgically generated by ceremonies imported from the Holy Sepulchre: in Jerusalem, Crusaders' processional liturgies began at the eastern altar and ended in the rotunda at the tomb.[14] Whether or not there were special ritual actions or a tomb proxy at the Round's center, the Temple's dual orientation referenced its archetype in Jerusalem. The indexical relationship between the model and its archetype is sustained by the identical inversion of their axes. In 1506, an English pilgrim to the Holy Land, Sir Richard Guildford, understood the Holy Sepulchre through its model in London: "The disposition and making of the Temple of the Holy Sepulchre is round at the west end and eastward formed after the making of a [normal, basilican] church, much after the form and making of the Temple at London, save it is far exceeding in greatness."[15] The Temple Church does not look like the Holy Sepulchre in Jerusalem, but it certainly acts like it. In the Middle Ages, those who desired the near presence of the site of Jesus's empty tomb sought not its appearance, but its physical, ritual experience. That force of the sacred was not located in the visual aspects of the building—its exterior form or its stylistic details. Its power was, rather, embedded in how the structure determined a believer's movement within it—by its plan and by the objects that were encountered.

The Temple Church was a model of the Holy Sepulchre for political reasons as well as pious ones. It signposted, publicly and prominently within the city, the interests of the most powerful military and economic religious order of the day, the Knights Templar.[16] In popular productions from Sir Walter Scott's novel *Ivanhoe* to Ubisoft's video game *Assassin's Creed*, the Knights Templar appear as brutal villains. At the other extreme, they are depicted as heroes. In Dan Brown's *The Da Vinci Code*, for example, they are celebrated as anti-Catholic urfeminists.[17] In scholarly literature the Templars are more soberly presented. They were Crusaders. Their order, identified as the Poor Fellow-Soldiers of Christ and of the Temple of Solomon (*Pauperes commilitones Christi Templique Salomonici*), was founded in Jerusalem two decades after Latin Christians conquered the Muslim city and slaughtered its inhabitants. Templars were the first of the Catholic Church's military monastic orders, established to protect pilgrims on their way to the Holy City.[18] The Templars are recognized as a dominant factor both in the Crusaders' military occupation of Palestine and in the funding of the West's wars in the East. Despite the poverty vowed by individual knights, the Templar order famously amassed a great deal of wealth. Indeed, the Templars have even been described as the protobankers of Europe.[19] Those riches came less from plunder than from rents and donations generated by their close ties both with the Holy Land and with the social elites of the West.[20] Templar knights were, it should be remembered, recruited exclusively from the aristocracy.

The Templars had a special relationship not only with Jerusalem but also with the Holy Sepulchre. According to their rule, if a Templar left his quarters in Jerusalem at night, it could only be to go to the Holy Sepulchre.[21] Along with the Knights of the Hospital, they held the keys of the treasury in the Holy Sepulchre in which the relic of the True Cross was kept. The Holy Sepulchre was the principal object of veneration of the pilgrims who the Templars were sworn to protect. The Temple Church's link to the Church of the Holy Sepulchre and to Jerusalem was enhanced at its dedication. "On the 10th of February in the year from the Incarnation of our Lord 1185, this Church was consecrated in honor of the Blessed Mary by the Lord Heraclius, by the grace of God Patriarch of the Church of the Holy Resurrection [the Church of the Holy Sepulchre], who, to those visiting it annually, granted an indulgence of sixty days off the penance enjoined upon them."[22] The structure's indexical relationship with the Church of the Holy Sepulchre was strengthened by its name, the officiant who dedicated it, and the indulgences it was accorded. Though officially dedicated to Mary, like many Templar sanctuaries, the London preceptory was always identified as "the Temple."[23] "Patriarch of the Church of the Holy Resurrection" was the title of the Patriarch of Jerusalem: the Sepulchre was the synecdoche of the city. Indulgences provided pious petitioners remission from suffering in purgatory for confessed and forgiven sins. They were earned by supporting good causes (like the Crusades) and by performing acts of devotion, including worship at particularly sacred sites, like that of the Holy Sepulchre in Jerusalem or St. Peter's in Rome.

The Temple Church's reference to the Holy Sepulchre also allowed it a share of its referent's significant political force. The building was not only a monumental surrogate of the Holy Sepulchre but an effective sign of its possessors—giving physical presence to a powerful fusion of social forces. The Templars persuasively deployed this sign as a means of confirming their military order's place of political privilege. The model performed as a totem, marking the territory of a clan that claimed a special relationship with its archetype and assumed its authority. The Temple also operated as a trophy, demonstrating the Templars' military ability to occupy the East and appropriate its forms. The Temple provocatively contributed to the new order in the urban fabric, presenting not only the sacrality of Jerusalem but also the institutional authority of the Templars. It was a powerful political model in the Middle Ages. But, if once it was a destination of knights, kings, and pilgrims, now it is a place of lawyers and tourists. In modernity, it has lost its referent. Many visitors think it is called the Temple Church after the eponymously named London Underground station nearby. Though the Temple Church's remarkable relation to the Holy Sepulchre may still be recognized by a few historians, for most of its observers it is no longer a model at all.

My discussion of the Temple Church as a medieval architectural model is premised on Richard Krautheimer's classic article of 1942, "Introduction to an 'Iconography of Medieval Architecture.'"[24] In that essay, Krautheimer brilliantly demonstrates that the identification of a copy with its archetype did not depend on mimetic resemblance, but rather on reproducing those bits of the archetype that signified most powerfully. He summarizes his argument: "The architect of a medieval copy did not intend to imitate the prototype as it looked in reality; he intended to reproduce it *typice* and *figuraliter* [typologically and figuratively], as a memento of a venerated site and simultaneously as a symbol of promised salvation."[25] But this observation, like any I make in this book, is a product of its particular historiographic moment: it betrays the assumptions of the time in which it was written. Questioning those assumptions further clarifies important aspects of medieval models. The characterization of the medieval copy as a "memento" is perhaps a symptom of a World War II nostalgia for a gentler past. "Memento" is both too personal and too seeped in Romanticism, like the cherished lock of hair of a lost lover. A medieval model of the Holy Sepulchre did not awaken the memory of an earlier experience of the Resurrection of Jesus. Rather, it rendered its promise of salvation always present. Krautheimer's privileging of the architect and his intentions as an independent author of a building is also anachronous. His use of "copy" for his subject raises further questions. The pious beholder, then as now, was less concerned with the appearance of the structure than with its essence—its revelation to humans of their relation to the divine and the ritual recreations of those interactions. As Krautheimer observed, medieval European models made of the Holy Sepulchre conveyed that essence through their appropriation of its name, its practices, and some of its formal attributes. But "copy" emphasizes an object's derivativeness and marks it as secondary. A copy of the *Mona Lisa* never has the force of the original. But medieval monumental models of the Holy Sepulchre were *surrogates* of their referent, not mere copies. They acted more like reproductions of the Bible and less like reproductions of the *Mona Lisa*. They made available the Holy Sepulchre's performative substance in a way that enhanced the spiritual and political standing of its patrons and of its site. These model surrogates reenacted the Holy Sepulchre in its rituals, its effects, and its privileges (e.g., indulgences). The original Holy Sepulchre in Jerusalem not only monumentalized the central tenet of Christianity—the Resurrection—but also celebrated its imperial patron, promoted its possessors' political status, and made Jerusalem a destination. Patrons of its medieval proxies—like the London Templars—had similar ambitions for their buildings.

The high medieval Temple Church exemplifies the macropolitics of building models in the European Middle Ages as well as demonstrating their indexical character. A second structure, the late medieval Rucellai tomb in Florence, both elaborates on that indexicality and reveals a micropolitics of models that augers modernity. The Rucellai Holy Sepulchre refers not to the whole of the Church of the Holy Sepulchre in Jerusalem, but only to its aedicule—the part of the building at the center of the Rotunda that enclosed the empty tomb, the central proof of Christianity's promise of everlasting life. The Florentine structure is small, about the size of a delivery van (fig. 14).[26] The model looks nothing like its archetype, but invokes its aura through exquisiteness. It is an elegantly proportioned rectangular block with a semicircular apse. The neat abstraction of its basic volumes is complemented by delicately carved Corinthian pilasters and a revetment of framed, square marble panels, each with an intricate intarsia medallion. Its clear geometric forms contrast with its lacy crown of lilies and its delicate lantern. The

FIG. 14. Florence, San Pancrazio, Chapel of the Holy Sepulchre. (Photograph by Sailko, Wikipedia Creative Commons, *https://commons.wikimedia.org/wiki/File:Tempietto_dell %27alberti_restaurato,_08.JPG*)

elegant Latin frieze inscription of inlaid black marble further accentuates the structure's refinement. The tomb speaks to its visitor, identifying itself as the place from whence Jesus rose from the dead:

> You are seeking Jesus of Nazareth who was crucified. He is risen; he is not here; behold the place where they put him. [Mark 16:6][27]

A second inscription, carved in a marble plaque over the small structure's only entrance, explicitly names both the monument's archetype and its patron:

> Johannes Rucellarius, son of Paulus, so that he might pray for his own salvation from the same source whence the resurrection of all has been accomplished with Christ, has arranged for this chapel to be built according to the likeness of the tomb in Jerusalem, 1467.[28]

The plaque establishes that Giovanni di Paolo Rucellai (1403–81), a prominent Florentine banker and patron of the arts, built this Holy Sepulchre so that his prayers would be as propitious coming from the chapel adjacent to his palace as they would be originating from Jerusalem. The model does not act as an urban marker of the status of an institution, as did the Temple Church. Rather, in its opulence, location, and religious authority, it signifies the elevated status of a wealthy individual: its politics are the micropolitics of the emerging mercantile elite. No mention is made of the Sepulchre's architect.

The master of the Rucellai Sepulchre was identified only a century after its construction in the publication in 1568 of the second edition of Giorgio Vasari's *Lives of the Most Eminent Painters, Sculptors and Architects*.[29] Vasari attributes the tomb to Leon Battista Alberti (1404–72), whom he disparages as a famous author but a second-rate architect. Art historians have long disagreed with Vasari's assessment of Alberti. Jacob Burckhardt, the nineteenth-century cultural historian who popularized the Renaissance, also popularized an exalted view of Alberti. For Burkhardt, Alberti embodied the ideal Renaissance man. He polished Alberti's image as great writer, painter, architect, and courtier to a high shine for an appreciative bourgeois audience who identified with Burckhardt's very male heroes:

> An acute and practiced eye might be able to trace, step by step, the increase in the number of complete men during the fifteenth century.... When this impulse to the highest individual development was combined with a powerful and varied nature, which had mastered all the elements of the culture of the age, then arose the "all-sided man"—*"l'uomo universale"*—who belonged to Italy alone.... Among these many-sided men, some who may truly be called all-sided, tower above the rest.... Consider for a moment the figure of one of these giants—Leon Battista Alberti.... It need not be added that an iron will pervaded and sustained his whole personality; like all the great men of the Renaissance, he said, "Men can do all things if they will."[30]

Burckhardt's assessment remains very much in place: Alberti "epitomized the Renaissance man," claims the first sentence of his entry in Wikipedia.[31]

Now, Alberti is universally acknowledged to be the designer of the Rucellai Holy Sepulchre; indeed, its association with Alberti has controlled its reception. The Sepulchre's identification as a thing produced by a great Renaissance artist helps explain what has been seen in it and what has remained hidden. Those features of the building understood as Albertian—its notional proportional systems and its motifs—have been investigated with forensic intensity. Alberti's engagement with music and mathematics is well documented.[32] As a consequence, the building's exterior has been obsessively measured and diagrammed.[33] A place has been made for the Rucellai Sepulchre in the Albertian paradigm and in the evolutionary scheme of modern architecture. Most important, because of its status as the work of a major Renaissance artist, the monument is conscientiously attended to by scholars, if not the public.

Those aspects of the work that do not fit the Albertian paradigm are commonly ignored or dismissed. For example, the tomb's anticlassical features, most marked in its off-axis entrance and its three-pilaster facade, are noted in scholarly literature only in passing, if at all. But, according to Alberti himself, no respectable sacred building would be caught dead with a three-column facade and a door to one side. Alberti's *De re aedificatoria,* written between 1443 and 1452, was the most important treatise on architecture published in the West since Vitruvius's *De architectura.*[34] In it, Alberti dictates, "The number of gaps between columns should be odd, the number of columns always even."[35] Indeed, by Alberti's own pronouncement, the arrangement of the Sepulchre's pilasters is unnatural: "Taking their example from Nature, [the ancients] never made the bones of the building, meaning the columns, angles, and so on, odd in number—for you will not find a single animal that stands or moves upon an odd number of feet. Conversely, they never made openings [between supports] even in number; this they evidently learned from Nature: to animals she has given ears, eyes and nostrils matching on either side, but in the centre, single and obvious, she has set the mouth."[36] The tomb's utter frustration of the Albertian rules of symmetry tends to be overlooked. Also absent from art historical notice is Giovanni di Paolo Rucellai's body. Most Renaissance tombs contain at least parts of their patrons, but the location of Giovanni's earthly remains is apparently unknown.[37]

The modelness of the Rucellai Holy Sepulchre is badly handled in the scholarly literature on the structure. Modern scholars seem discomfited by the miniature building's claim to be the Holy Sepulchre. Most have commented on the copy's lack of mimetic reference to its archetype in Jerusalem. Commonly mentioned is the "fact" that the Rucellai tomb is only about half the size of its referent. Apart from a few details—the marble cladding of the structure, a crowning lantern, an apsidal end—art historians identify very few features of the Jerusalem aedicule in the Rucellai tomb. But the Florentine model's lack of similarity to the Holy Sepulchre requires some explanation. One symptomatic account of the difference has found resonance: the Renaissance Rucellai Sepulchre was an improvement of the medieval original. Ludwig Heydenreich, a prominent German art historian and director of the Kunsthistorisches Institut in Florence during World War II, argues that the Florentine Sepulchre was a conscious idealization based on early Christian sources of the contemporary structure in Jerusalem.[38] This fantasy is replayed in later literature. The Renaissance architectural historian Robert Tavenor remarks: "It is half the size and a geometrically 'perfected' interpretation of the Holy Sepulchre in Jerusalem. Such improvements were necessary because, by Quattrocento standards, the Holy Sepulchre had been badly built, with irregularities in its formal geometry."[39] Arguments like these assume that the archetype was known well enough to be thought ugly. A mimetically correct imitation could have been made, but for aesthetic reasons was not. Indeed, these authors refer to a letter written by Giovanni di Paola Rucellai to his mother indicating that he had sent agents to Jerusalem to take measurements of Jesus's tomb.[40] In the 1970s, Francis William Kent, however, conclusively demonstrated that this letter is a fake, probably of the eighteenth century.[41]

A reconsideration of the Rucellai tomb as a production of the Middle Ages rather than the Renaissance provides insight into both the form of the monument and the function of its august archetype (the weak model becomes the strong one). Here both form and function are enacted in the particularities of medieval computation. Measurements were certainly central to the indexical power of the Rucellai tomb, but those measurements were of a very different nature than those of modernity. In the middle of the fifteenth century the understanding in the West of the form of the Holy Sepulchre still largely depended, as it had in the Middle Ages, on textual descriptions, not images. Renaissance scholars who look exclusively at the exterior of the Rucellai tomb find it utterly unlike its referent. They have missed the essential similarity of its interior to that of its referent (fig. 15).[42] The structure encloses a single space—the tomb chamber—occupied on one side by a marble-encased credenza-like mensa tomb. The size of that chamber in Florence (approximately 2.76 m × 1.76 m) is remarkably close in size to that of the tomb chamber in Jerusalem (approximately 2.38 m × 2.30 m). Like its referent in Jerusalem, the mensa tomb in the Rucellai tomb takes up almost half of the width of the interior, requiring the entrance to be decentered to the far left. The opening into the tomb chamber is, in both cases, a similar height, requiring those who enter it to bend down. It was the interior of the tomb in Jerusalem's Holy Sepulchre that was and still is the object of pilgrims' veneration. It is that part of

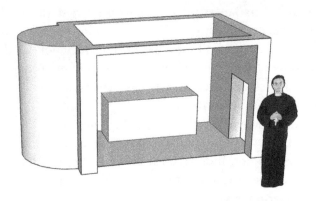

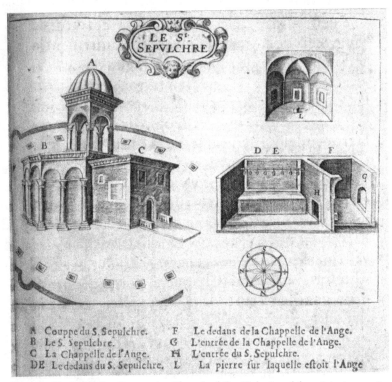

FIG. 15. Florence, San Pancrazio, Chapel of the Holy Sepulchre, interior cavity. SketchUp model by the author compared with the section of the Holy Sepulchre in Jerusalem by Louis Deshayes de Courmenin, *Voiage de Levant fait par le commandement du Roy en l'année 1621 par le Sr D. C.* (Paris: A. Taupinart, 1645), 399. (David M. Rubenstein Rare Book and Manuscript Library, Duke University)

the aedicule—understood as the place in which the bodily remains of God rested for three days—that medieval pilgrims piously measured with strings and ribbons which then became blessings, *eulogia*, and relics, *sacra*. Daniel the Russian Abbot (fl. early twelfth century) provides an example of such a measuring. Having first deposited in the Holy Sepulchre an unlit lamp where Jesus's feet would have lain and then, witnessing the annual miracle of the Holy Fire on Holy Saturday, Daniel returns to collect his now burning lamp: "Bowing down before the holy tomb and kissing with love and tears the holy place where the most pure body of Our Lord Jesus Christ lay, I then measured the tomb in length and breadth and height, for when people are present it is quite impossible to measure it."[43]

Some sense of what happened to those ribbon measures and relics in the mid-fifteenth century is also offered by pilgrims' accounts. The bizarre Margery Kempe gifted ribbon measures in return for hospitality offered to her during her return from Jerusalem. "And as it happened, she was in lodgings in a good man's house, and many neighbors came in to encourage her in her perfection and her holiness—and she gave them the measurement of Christ's grave, which they received very piously, taking great joy in it and thanking her very much for it."[44] More remarkable is the inventory of a Holy Sepulchre chapel in the Augustinian Priory of Bonhommes at Edington in Wiltshire, which was dedicated by an English pilgrim to Jerusalem: William Wey, a contemporary of Giovanni di Paolo Rucellai. Among the many items from his pilgrimage to Palestine that Wey left in the chapel were "other things of the holy land made in panels [bordys]. First in a panel [borde] behind the choir the length of our Lord's sepulchre, with the height of the door, the breadth of the door, the length of our Lord's foot, the depth of the mortice of the cross and the roundness of the same."[45] The tomb chamber in Jerusalem was the *locus* that was recorded in texts and numbers; it was that internal space that mattered. And this *locus* was the referent of the Rucellai tomb model. Measurements in late antiquity and the Middle Ages made of sacred spaces were themselves *sacra*: the length of the slab on which the dead Jesus was laid, the distance between the tomb and Golgotha, the height of the door into the tomb chamber. Measurements were not made of a building's plan.

In modern scholarship, the distinction between measuring *sacra* and measuring buildings is sometimes overlooked.[46] These contact measurements give to models of the Middle Ages that material adjacency so central to Peirce's understanding of the index: the Rucellai tomb is related to its referent in Jerusalem not mimetically, but indexically.[47]

Like other medieval models of the Holy Sepulchre, the Rucellai tomb's indexical relation to its referent in Jerusalem was established by the duplication of its practices and meanings as well as by the measurements of its *sacra*. That it behaved like its archetype is demonstrated by Pope Paul II's bull of 1471. The bull granted those who "prayed at the foot of the shrine" on Good Friday and Easter Sunday an indulgence of five years.[48] The Rucellai Holy Sepulchre's architectural identity was established by its naming and by its interior measurements. Authorship was ascribed to a patron rather than to an architect. As is the case with most other medieval copies, the master who designed and built the Rucellai tomb went unnamed in the monument's inscriptions and in its contemporary documentation. The Rucellai Sepulchre thus fits neatly into the medieval and late medieval paradigm of Holy Sepulchre models. It might even be claimed that the Rucellai tomb is one of the last of the significant medieval reproductions of its sacred referent. Embedded in that assertion is the model's place in the micropolitics of academic disciplinary competition: a medievalist's critique of the "Renaissance."

Icon: Early Modern Building Model

In the Middle Ages, the *visual* resemblance of a model to its referent meant very little; later, appearance was everything. An early modern model of the Holy Sepulchre, now in the British Museum (BM 10339), demonstrates a transformation of the model from indexical to iconic (fig. 16).[49] The political and technological developments that enabled that model's making help explain not only its dramatic change of form but also the broader cultural shift in representation that occurred in the early modern West.

The model is a delightful object, about the size of a small carry-on bag. It is made of polished olive and pistachio wood inlaid with

Fig. 16. London, British Museum, model of the Holy Sepulchre (BM 10339), exterior from the "south." (Courtesy of the British Museum)

elaborate mother-of-pearl ornament and articulated with camel bone columns and archivolts. No surface goes undecorated. Small floriated crosses are distributed evenly across simple surfaces and with greater density at edges to emphasize structure, for example on the corners of the bell tower. Larger planes have border inlays or ornamental roundels. Two such panels, prominently located at the front of the structure, are decorated emblematically: the Jerusalem cross ornaments the entrance piazza and the Name of Jesus (IHS) in a sunburst embellishes the base of the bell tower. The small scale of the structure, the glowing polish of its dark wood, and its dense iridescent ornament gives it the appearance of a large and elaborate jewel box. Like a jewel box, the model opens up to reveal its treasures.[50] These treasures are not, however, precious stones, but further openings. The model is not, after all, a jewel box, but a puzzle box: hidden chambers are revealed by removing roofs and ceilings, opening miniature doors and sliding out tiny dividers. The model's manipulator explores it somatically, like a pilgrim explores the Holy Sepulchre. The rich confusions of the space are slowly revealed as the seeker's eyes and hand (rather than the pilgrim's eyes and body) probe its various parts. At the core is the miniature empty Sepulchre of Jesus, disclosed upon the removal of its aedicule's tiny cupola. The model allows not just an understanding of the building's complexity, but also the haptic and even psychological experience of that complexity's discovery. It offers the topography of the sacred site, a surrogate pilgrimage. This model of the Holy Sepulchre allows its possessor to experience the physical confusion of its archetype.

The British Museum model of the Holy Sepulchre is one of a series of similar but never identical models of the Holy Sepulchre crafted by Roman Catholic Palestinian artisans in Bethlehem from the end of the sixteenth century to the beginning of the eighteenth. About thirty of these models have been published; others may still be hidden in private collections and ecclesiastical repositories; many have been lost.[51] These small, early modern models of the Holy Sepulchre acted very differently than did the medieval monumental models of the shrine. Those structures provided a public and performative presence of a particularly powerful absence; they invited communal rather than individual participation in the enactment of a distant sacred place. Before modernity, in models like the Temple Church, the *collective* rituals of Holy Sepulchres in the West reinforced their identification with the Holy Sepulchre. The visual resemblance of the model to its archetype was inessential not only because the appearance of the original was unknown to its users but also because of the participatory understanding of its meaning. In contrast to the shared experience of a monumental, public enactment of the Holy Sepulchre, models like that in the British Museum presented a private, elite experience of a scrupulously rendered miniature of the holy site.

These icons of the Holy Sepulchre may be jewel-like puzzle boxes, but they are also carefully scaled models of their archetype. A drawing by Gustaf Dalman of the longitudinal section of one of these models compared with that of the Holy Sepulchre itself exemplifies their identicality.[52] Inside and out, the model miniaturizes the volumes of its referent with remarkable exactitude. Greater precision was hardly possible in an age before mechanical, then digital, instruments enabled reproduction. These models would not, however, have been possible without one new technology: measured drawings. A chief advocate and successful popularizer of measured drawings was Leon Battista Alberti, ironically the same man identified with designing one of the last medieval Holy Sepulchres. In his *De re aedificatoria*, Alberti recommends making measured drawings and models of classical works as an essential preparation for an architect. The centrality of measured drawings to Alberti's practice is evidenced in his many references to them.[53] An architect, he observes, must test and refine his own designs by making and remaking drawings and models.[54] Once perfected, those drawings could be sent to a distant site to be entrusted to competent laborers capable of following the architect's "precise instructions." For Alberti, "precise instructions" along with "sound advice" were all that could be legitimately demanded of an architect by his patron. He assumed that the architect did not need to be present at the building site; he even seems to warn against it: "Should you propose to supervise and execute the work, you will hardly be able to avoid having sole responsibility for all the errors and mistakes committed by others."[55] Better to appoint a competent site manager (*adstitores*) who would be constantly present.[56]

Drawn models are the means by which the architect not only distinguishes himself from the master mason, but also removes himself from the messiness of the building site. In the Middle Ages, the designer was a master mason who worked on site, adapting the form and details of his building to circumstances as they changed during construction.[57] He both conceived the structure and built it. In modernity, the architect replaced the master mason. Alberti provided the protocol for this shift. The architect designed the building; contractors and laborers constructed it. Essential to the separation of an architect from the material enactment of his work was the perfection of his design and the graphic means of presenting it to those who would build it. Earlier than in many other parts of the economy, the division of labor breached architecture. In *De re aedificatoria* the absent designer replaces the present one; immediacy is displaced by detachment. The personal, on-site authority of the medieval master mason is usurped by the impersonal disciplinary authority of the architect's drawn or built models. The perfected building is more fully expressed in those than in their final, built form. The architect composes the strong model of a weak building. Alberti the author makes Alberti the architect authorial: just as the writer assumes control of the text, so the architect assumes control of the building. The architectural historian Mario Carpo describes the novelty of Alberti's practice, emphasizing its effects with his italics: "In Alberti's theory, *the design of the building is the original and the building is its copy.*"[58]

"It is a scientific platitude that there can be neither precise control nor prediction of phenomena without measurement."[59] Objective measurement, understood as the basis for Modern science, was also the basis for the exacting reproduction of buildings. The architect's idea of a building can be reproduced at a distance if all its measurements are presented to her contractor; equally, an existing building (like one of the temples drawn and measured by Alberti) could be replicated by capturing its dimensions. But architectural iconicity depends on more than numbers and formal replication. It also requires recognition. For a model to function mimetically, its users or observers, as well as its makers, must be aware that it *looks* like its referent. Iconicity necessitates the broad circulation of images of the archetype as well as the availability of its plans and sections. Iconicity did not come with the invention of the printing press in 1440 (as the Rucellai Holy Sepulchre demonstrates), but only later with its broad popularization.[60] Western models of the Holy Sepulchre that were understood to look like their archetype were not possible before the technology of graphic reproduction enabled the broad distribution of its representations. The extensive circulation of images necessary for effective mimesis was only fully operational in the sixteenth century. The effect of both technologies—architectural measurement and widespread replication—are perfectly embodied in the model of the Holy Sepulchre in the British Museum.

This British Museum Holy Sepulchre model dates from sometime before 1753, when it came to the British Museum as part of that institution's founding bequest by Hans Sloane.[61] Although, like most other members of the series, the British Museum model is impossible to date with precision, the measured drawings which enabled its making are not. Plans and elevations of the Holy Sepulchre were drawn by Bernardino Amico between 1593 and 1597.[62] They were later published in Europe by Raimondi in 1609, under the title *Trattato delle piante et imagini de i sacri edificii di Terra Santa;* a second edition, with the plates executed by the recognized master of the craft, Jacques Callot, appeared in 1620.[63] Most publications by Western travelers to the Holy Land were narrative accounts of their adventure; if there were images, they only accessorized the text. In contrast, in Amico's extraordinary volume, texts are mere supplements to the images. The work represents fifteen sites in the Holy Land with nearly fifty plates, each of which is accompanied by an explanatory chapter. Amico deals with the Holy Sepulchre in particular detail, devoting eleven plates to the monument (fig. 17). Through these images and their textual appendages,

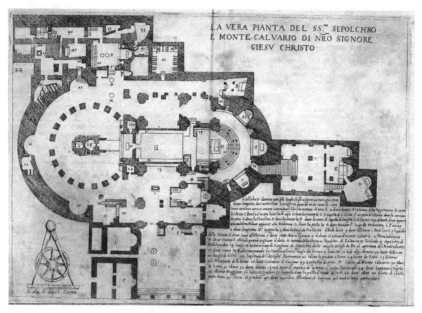

Fig. 17. Jerusalem, Church of the Holy Sepulchre, plan. Bernardino Amico, *Trattato*, 2nd ed., pl. 22.

the author accompanies the reader in an exploration of the building: "Walking along the gallery of the Dome you go by the stairs of our [the Franciscans'] place marked number 48 [in the plan], to a small door which opens in the middle of the gallery to the north, and having reached there, you can then walk everywhere: to the east you find a door cut out in the very wall of the big arch, which is reached by two stairs" (fig. 18).[64] As a means of conveying the substance of the building Amico deployed plans, elevations, and sections with exact measurements and scales. He introduced figures into the drawings with whom readers might identify as they moved about the building through its images. Amico also marshaled various sophisticated perspective devices. "The Transparent Body" of the Tomb of the Virgin is, for example, a tour-de-force perspectival figuration of the underground space of the shrine.[65] Amico sought a more persuasively haptic expression of the holy sites' *realia*. His *Trattato*'s scaled measurements of the Holy Land's monuments (and not just their *sacra*) allowed physically compelling replicas to be made. In an exercise in Albertian principles,

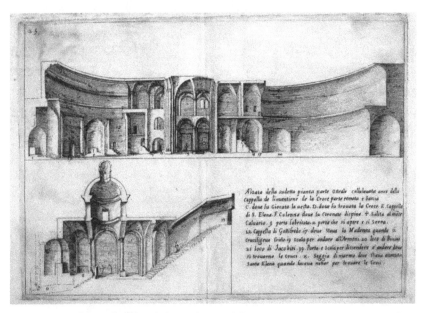

FIG. 18. Jerusalem, Church of the Holy Sepulchre, panoramic section. Bernardino Amico, *Trattato*, 2nd ed., pl. 25.

the *Trattato* enables true "portraits" (as Amico named them) of the Holy Sepulchre to be reproduced in the West. Indeed, Amico explains his elaborate representation of the Holy Sepulchre in terms of reproduction: "With regard to the plan of the Most Holy Sepulchre of Our Lord, I have not wished anything to be lacking, for the consolation of simple artisans who wish to reproduce it for others, so that they can do so with facility, making use of the scale, from which they can find every detail."[66]

Amico's measurements allowed the shrines' reproduction not only as distant monuments, but also as local miniatures. Certainly, the models' dependence on Amico's measurements is suggested by the similarity of the three-dimensional reproductions to their two-dimensional archetype.[67] Given the difference in media, their resemblance is formidable. The Italian archaeologist Bellarmino Bagatti has argued persuasively that the production of olive wood models in Bethlehem was begun under Amico's direction and with his drawings.[68] Not only did both the drawings and the replicas have the same source, but they also shared the organization that sustained them, the audiences to which they were directed, and the political acts that they were meant to perform.

The organization underwriting both the *Trattato* and the olive wood models was the great Catholic mendicant order established in 1209 by Saint Francis of Assisi, the Franciscans. In the sixteenth century, the Franciscans were the only licit representatives of the West with a role in the care of Christian holy sites of Palestine. After the final collapse of the Crusader Kingdom with the fall of Acre in 1291, the Latins only possessed parts of the Christian holy sites by buying them. In the fourteenth century, the Angevin kings purchased from Palestine's overlords, the Mamluks, rights to segments of some of the principal shrines of the Holy Land, most notably the Cenacle on Mount Zion (traditionally identified as the site of the Last Supper), the Holy Sepulchre in Jerusalem, and the Church of the Nativity in Bethlehem.[69] These rights were awarded to the Franciscans, who, like their Templar predecessors, were tasked with providing for Western (Catholic and, later, also Protestant) pilgrims who visited the holy places. In Bethlehem, the Franciscans were also responsible for the community of

Palestinian Catholics who produced the olive wood models of sacred places. Those shrines in the Holy Land became the Franciscans' cultural capital—the basis, for example, of their control of the popular Stations of the Cross in Roman Catholic churches.[70] Bernardino Amico was a Franciscan of the Custody in Palestine.

The displacement of the Mamluks and establishment of Ottoman sovereignty in Jerusalem in 1517 was good for most Jerusalemites, but not for the Franciscan Custody. Franciscans lost access to the shrine of the Ascension on the Mount of Olives and the Cenacle on Mount Zion. Further, the Greek Orthodox, as a recognized people native to the Ottoman Empire, pressed for the eviction of the foreign Franciscans from the Church of the Nativity and the Holy Sepulchre. The northern European Protestant threat to Catholicism also affected the status of the Holy Places and of the Franciscans who occupied them. In medieval, largely illiterate communities of the medieval Latin West, texts were, of course, essential to religious practice, but texts shared their authority with more popularly accessible, material vehicles of divine will—priests, rituals, images, relics, and sacred places. Traditional Christianities continue to honor those ancient habits. Early Modern Protestants, however, accorded language—texts and sermons—an undisputed primacy as the medium for understanding God's plans for the world. The Protestant project was underwritten by the printing press, ubiquitous by the sixteenth century. Protestants scorned pilgrimage to the Holy Land or to anywhere else.[71] Most Protestants in early modernity (and still now) despised the Holy Sepulchre for its idolatrous images, incense, rituals, and priests.[72] They raised objections to its authenticity, sanctimoniously observing that the Gospel text explicitly locates the death and burial of Jesus outside the city walls. The present Holy Sepulchre, being within the walls, could not then be genuine. The Custody's treasure of sacred sites was, for Protestants, worthless. The early modern period—the age of the Reformation and Counter-Reformation—witnessed a significant decline in the number of pilgrims to the Holy Land.[73]

In different ways, both the olive wood models of the Holy Sepulchre and Amico's renderings responded to crises of the time: Ottoman threats to Franciscan properties and Protestant attacks on pilgrimage, along with the doubts that those virulent critiques raised among faithful Catholics. The models' exquisite ornament encoded their mission: the site's prestige was evoked by the precious materiality and devoted labor expended on its mother-of-pearl inlay and lovingly crafted bone colonettes and archivolts.[74] Their decoration also insisted on the Franciscan's control of the place. The objects announce themselves as Franciscan through the conspicuous display of insignia, like the Name of Jesus, associated with the order.[75] The Jerusalem cross, symbol of the Crusades, was also prominently emblazoned both on the coat of arms of the Franciscan Custody and on the Holy Sepulchre models. The most recognizable emblem of the Franciscans, the crossed arms and stigmatized hands of Jesus and Francis with a central cross, found on the Custody's seal, takes the place of the Holy Name in a number of the Holy Sepulchre models. Made by the Franciscans' Christian Palestinian parishioners, these models were thus "signed" by the Franciscan Custody.[76] The emblems are marks of authorship.

The models' decoration clearly identifies their patrons; it also locates their recipients. The cost of these olive wood Holy Sepulchres was significant—their possessors were members of the elite. The languages which are inscribed—mainly Latin and Italian—on the objects indicates that those elites were Western Europeans. Pious voyagers to Palestine certainly purchased smaller items made in the workshops of Bethlehem. Crosses, rosaries, and small statues were sold to pilgrims in the markets of Bethlehem and Jerusalem in early modernity as they are today. But the elaborate building models like that in the British Museum were apparently made primarily for export. How the Franciscans marketed the products of their craftsmen-parishioners in Bethlehem is suggested by Cornelio Magni, a Catholic traveler in the Holy Land in the later seventeenth century. He writes of the Catholic Palestinians of Bethlehem: "They are employed [by the Franciscans] for the most part making sacred things, such as crowns, crosses, models of the Holy Sepulchre, and many make these churches with great mastery, and noble ornament, of mother of pearl, ivory and others materials, producing good profits; these works are bought truly at a dear price, and sent throughout the Christian world."[77] The models' ornament occasionally allows us to know for whom they were intended. A number of the models of the Holy Sepulchre are adorned with the coats of arms of nobility as well as with Franciscan insignia. There is, in the collection of the Monastery of St. Ursula in Valetta on Malta, a model with the coat of arms of João V of Portugal (1706–50); another Holy Sepulchre, now in Lisbon, was apparently originally intended for England, as it bears the English royal coat of arms and the date 1661.[78] By far the most elaborate of the models meant for monarchs is now found in the Kunsthistorisches Museum in Vienna. Depicted on the bell tower of this model of the Holy Sepulchre are portraits of the Hapsburgs: Maria Teresa (1717–80), Francesco I, and their heir, Joseph.[79] The coats of arms and portraits decorating these Holy Sepulchres do not perform as signatures. They do not signify authorship, as do the Franciscan emblems. Rather, they act like imperial images on coins, declaring possession. They mark the site of the Holy Sepulchre in Jerusalem as already part of their domain.

The two-dimensional models of the *Trattato*, like the three-dimensional olive wood models that they informed, refine an appreciation of models' agency. Amico's work in Jerusalem was an aggressive response both to local Ottoman authority and to distant Protestant attacks on Jerusalem's shrines and on pilgrimage more broadly. His publications worked to establish the efficacy of pilgrimage by demonstrating the authenticity of its destinations. Two of the plates in his book directly address the Protestant accusations of inauthenticity directed against the Holy Sepulchre. Both a landscape view of Golgotha and the tomb cave and a "True Plan of the Ancient City of Jerusalem" show the sites of the crucifixion and burial as outside the city walls.[80] The images reinforce the claims made by Franciscan antiquarians that it was the city wall that moved, not the site of the crucifixion and burial.[81] More forcefully than scholarly texts, the visual argument was circulated in drawings. Catholic images as well as Protestant texts made use of the printing press. More fundamentally, Amico's *Trattato* attempts to prove the authenticity of the sites in the Holy Land by evoking their historical materiality—the physical intimacy of the shrines with God. The volume's plates act as models of the holy sites that they represented, pleading the case for their reliability as material witnesses to God's earthly existence. They testify through the exactness of their representation that the sacred spaces of Jerusalem are the *realia* of Jesus's own life. Jerusalem was not only the ideal city on the hill beloved by Protestants, but also a physical, historical place where physical, historical structures witnessed God's presence. Amico labored to offer his Western reader an intimate experience of the Eastern site through an iconic participation in sacred space.

The general charge of the Amico's drawings was to counter Protestant claims about the illegitimacy of the holy sites and reinforce Catholic faith in their efficacy. The last chapter in the *Trattato* suggests that the images of the shrines of the Holy Land were meant not only as passive stand-ins for experience, but also as active goads to a direct encounter with the sites. They were meant to stimulate pilgrimage. They were not a way to remember the Holy Land, but rather the means of anticipating a direct personal connection with the shrines. More aggressively, they were also published to provoke a new crusade to the Holy Land to recover the holy sites for the Catholic West. Amico makes this clear in the treatise's second edition. In its dedication to Cosimo II of Tuscany, Amico likens himself to Peter the Hermit, who inspired the First Crusade of 1099. He laments that Christians are more badly treated in the Holy Land than they were when Peter urged its conquest: "Today our Fathers and the pilgrims suffer a thousand times more, for not only are they ill-treated . . . and what is worse, and which is more important, the holy places possessed by them have been taken from us. . . . I sketched the true and real portraits of those most sacred places . . . for the universal benefit of Christendom and in order to excite and enflame the minds and hearts of Catholic Princes for the recovery of the Holy Land."[82] Amico describes the dangers that imperiled the friars and pilgrims in the Holy Land. More specifically, he laments the Franciscans' loss of control of the Cenacle on Mount Zion, the site of the Last Supper. To remedy the situation, he calls for war. Amico hopes that his images, like Colin Powell's slide identifying "an Iraqi aluminum tube for uranium enrichment," will inspire a new crusade.[83] The idea of a crusade to regain the Holy Land was familiar enough in early modernity. Columbus believed that the wealth generated by his voyages of discovery should be used to fund a new crusade and Paul III's *Laetare Hierusalem* (*Rejoice Jerusalem*), the bull issued in 1544 summoning the great Council of Trent, called for a crusade against the infidel Turks.[84] Amico's *Trattato* makes explicit how his models—both the two-dimensional ones in his book and the three-dimensional ones made in Bethlehem—were meant to act as agents of the Franciscans in the courts of Europe. Their mission was to rekindle the recipients' love of the holy places in Palestine and ignite a passion for their repossession.

The early modern drawings and olive wood models of the Holy Sepulchre nuance an understanding of models in general. Most critically for my argument they demonstrate the politicalness of models. These models had a role in the international macropolitics of early modernity. But they also demonstrate both the independence of models and their historicity. One example of their autonomy and another of the dramatic shifts in their interpretation should make these two attributes clear. The Holy Sepulchre models did not always do the Franciscans' political bidding. An anecdotal reference, entered under the year 1676 in the *Acta S. Congregationis de Propaganda Fide pro Terra Sancta*, suggests that they had the capacity to act in ways contrary to the interests of their producers. The episode comes from a particularly charged moment in the bitter struggle between the Greek Orthodox and the Franciscans for control of the Holy Sepulchre. Bishop Ridolfi, the Italian patriarchal vicar of Constantinople, reported on a secret meeting of the Greek patriarch with the Ottoman council of the Grand Vizier Köprülüzade Fazıl Ahmed Pasha. The Greek ecclesiastic had with him one of the Franciscan models of the Church of the Holy Sepulchre, "which was opened to show all the parts [of the church], with the intention of arguing that the Holy Sepulchre was occupied always by his nation, including the arch of the choir [*gran cuba*], Calvary, the Column of the Flagellation and other parts, and that the Latins had never been masters and only officiated where the Greeks permitted them."[85] Here the autonomous agency of a Franciscan model is demonstrated by its anti-Franciscan behavior.

In early modernity, the Franciscan olive wood models were powerful agents of piety and politics; now they are not. As products of particular social conditions, they are obviously historical, but their historical condition is perhaps most apparent in the dramatic loss of their original authority. Whatever other jobs they had had, these models also multitasked as relics. Like a relic, a model participates in the aura of its source and performs for its possessor as a surrogate for its referent. Sacredness clings to relics. In modernity, instead of contributing to the strength of the model as it did from the late sixteenth to the eighteenth centuries, the models' conspicuously relic-like character, along with their small size and decorative form, exiled them from the category of "fine arts," and sequestered them among the decorated mirrors, embellished armor, and porcelain figurines of the minor arts.[86] Consequently, although these models of the Holy Sepulchre were powerful in early modernity, they are weak now. A few, tucked away with elaborately embroidered vestments and empty reliquaries in church treasuries, may retain something of their religious status. But most are regarded as mere curiosities and identified, in both popular and scholarly literature, as "souvenirs." The British Museum model, for example, is named "souvenir" in the title of a useful and learned article published by the institution that possesses it.[87] An advertisement by a high-end antiquities dealer typifies the popular understanding of these models:

> In 1335 the Franciscans returned to [Jerusalem] and numerous churches, monasteries and their associated hospices were built to care for and accommodate the thousands of Christian pilgrims. The opportunities for tourism that this influx presented was immense and this model is an elaborate, exotic and costly example of a souvenir made to satisfy the still vital pilgrimage market of the 17th century because by then the holy city had also became an important Grand Tour destination for the wealthy Princes and aristocracy of Europe.[88]

This passage is hopelessly full of historical errors—the use of "souvenir" is one of them. The term is subtly dismissive. It identifies the model as a mere commodity. Relics cannot be legally bought or sold; souvenirs are made for the market. In the twentieth and twenty-first centuries souvenirs are broadly understood to be cheap, portably small components of bulk travel and mass production. Certainly the value of a souvenir, like that of a relic, lies principally in how adequately it conveys its referent to its possessor. But in contrast to a relic, which has a communally acknowledged meaning, the souvenir's effectiveness is limited to the individual whose memory it evokes. It is a personal thing. Certainly, some of these fine olive wood and mother-of-pearl models acted like an elite sort of souvenir, bought by wealthy travelers as an *aide-mémoire,* but even those would, in early modernity, powerfully represent their possessor's experience of the sacred.

The relic-like models made in Bethlehem, computationally scaled to their referent, but distinctly decorated as objects-in-themselves, functioned as iconic agents for their producers. They were quintessentially early modern. In modernity, like the Temple Church in London, they lost their effectiveness. Now these olive wood and mother-of-pearl Holy Sepulchres are demoted to souvenirs and curiosities. Some of these models are found in museum collections, but these are rarely if ever displayed (the British Museum, in this as in many other ways, is different). Where models are on permanent exhibition, their museum hosts are usually either comatose (the Rockefeller Museum in Jerusalem) or nonelite, filled with vitrines of pottery, metalwork, and old apparel (the Museum of the Order of St. John in London).[89] Those in lively museums with superb art collections sometimes disappear altogether, leaving behind only digital residue.[90]

Analog: Modern Building Model

In Jerusalem, the height occupied by the Holy Sepulchre competed with the height of the Temple Mount. Height is power. Height is coveted by elites as well as armies. Height defines social status as well as topography: aristocracies are elevated. In premodernity, height was effectively fortified; it still facilitates surveillance. Height abets the manifestation of force; those who occupy the heights commonly supplement their dominance through construction, monumentalizing their authority. Where a height is absent, it may well be produced—like the ziggurats of Mesopotamia or the battle castles of sea-faring war galleys. The Temple Church created a height on the bank of the Thames. The real, material advantage of overseeing subsidizes the rapture of the panoramic gaze. Michel de Certeau famously describes that form of visual ecstasy:

> To be lifted to the summit of the World Trade Center is to be lifted out of the city's grasp.... An Icarus flying above these waters, he can ignore the devices of Daedalus in mobile and endless labyrinths far below. His elevation transfigures him into a voyeur. It puts him at a distance. It transforms the bewitching world by which one was "possessed" into a text that lies before one's eyes. It allows one to read it, to be a solar Eye, looking down like a god. The exaltation of a scopic and gnostic drive: the fiction of knowledge is related to this lust to be a viewpoint and nothing more.[91]

It feels so very good to be in control, de Certeau suggests, even if control is an illusion. The viewer looking down on New York from the top of one of the World Trade Center towers revels in the "fiction of knowledge" of a city miniaturized by distance.

Actual miniaturization bears with it some of the same gratifications of power provided by height. We almost always look down on miniatures. But the sense of control offered by a miniature to its possessor is not inevitably an illusion.[92] After all, the life of a toy truck is at the mercy of the child who plays with it. Models (and not just scale models), like miniatures, combine realities of power with their illusion. The ambiguities of phantom and factual authority are particularly apparent in modern urban models. They tend to fix fabulous pasts that are fictional (like the great model of imperial Rome constructed as part of Mussolini's archaeological exhibition celebrating the bimillennium of the birth of Emperor Augustus) or promise brilliant futures that contribute to a dystopic presence (like General Motors' Futurama in New York's 1939 World's Fair). Though they may be presented as benign edutainment, city models are a rich source for the recovery of the historical thinking of the time of their production, and, more important in this context, for the acknowledgment of the political function of modern architectural models in general. Jerusalem offers a perfect specimen of a modern analog model of a city's ancient version of itself (fig. 19).[93] It demonstrates how a model is historical and political;

FIG. 19. Jerusalem, model of ancient Jerusalem, view from the south. In the background is the Crown Plaza Hotel (originally the Hilton Hotel designed by Ya'acov Rechter). (Photograph by the author)

it also suggests how both its history and its politics are unstable and interdependent.

At a scale of 1:50, the model represents the walled city of Jerusalem at the brief moment of its greatest glory, between the time of the completion of Herod's Temple in 63/64 CE and its destruction by the Romans under the command of Titus during the First Jewish Revolt less than a decade later, in 70 CE. It is also Jerusalem at the time of Jesus. The model reproduces the topography of the ancient city, manifesting the manner in which monuments controlled and enhanced its heights. Most prominent is the great platform constructed by Herod to exaggerate the prominence of northeastern hill: the site of the old temple was aggrandized for the new one. The model's Herodian temple precinct, like the referent which it imagines, is more elaborately crafted than all but the most elite structures of the city. Jerusalem stone is used in the construction of all the buildings, but the Temple and palaces also deploy marble for details, miniature ceramic tiles for the roofs, and true gold leaf for its adornments. The detailing of the major monuments is exquisite; even the generic domestic dwellings are adorable. It is a persuasive recreation of the ancient city. Of what it persuades has shifted from when it was made to now. A model's politics are informed by its location. Initially the model was offered to the public in 1966 in the not-so-elite company of a mini-golf course, swimming pool, tennis courts, and bar at the Holy Land Hotel in Bayit Vagan, a western suburb about four miles from Jerusalem. Sixty years later the model moved to the salubrious precincts of the Israel Museum, next to the Shrine of the Book, in the neighborhood of the Knesset and the Hilton Hotel (now the Crowne Plaza) on the heights of Givat Ram West of the Old City of Jerusalem.

The "Holy Land Hotel Model of Ancient Jerusalem" was commissioned by the owner of the Holy Land Hotel, Hans Zvi Kroch. Michael Avi-Yonah, a distinguished senior Israeli archaeologist, agreed to oversee its construction; after 1974, the project was supervised by another esteemed archaeologist, Yoram Tsafrir.[94] At the time of its making, the model embodied the West's trust in scientific facticity and Cartesian order: the model was a body of research, a conscientiously gathered archive of a distant past. The model's guide book explains:

> The Model of Ancient Jerusalem . . . enables the visitor to study the city of Jerusalem at the time of the Second Temple. . . . The model is based on information derived from contemporary sources. Most important is the Jewish historian Flavius Josephus, a native of Jerusalem. Much information is found in the New Testament and in Jewish sources—the Mishna, the Tosephta and the Talmuds. The archaeological monuments and the excavations in various parts of Jerusalem are also indispensable sources of knowledge. Local traditions about the location of holy sites in Jerusalem were also taken into account.[95]

The model works hard to be as correct as possible. Ancient texts and scientific archaeological excavations establish this representation of Jerusalem in the first century CE as committed to truth telling. Like the texts and excavations on which it depends, the model is, for its makers, an object of "study." But this model, like all models, presents its version of veracity only through such deceptions as abstraction, suggestion, and allusion. Viewers of course understand that it is only an approximation. Where are the garbage dumps and slaughterhouses? Discussions of any model's "authenticity" are curiously off the mark.[96] The last sentence of the quote from the guidebook even points to the subjectivity of the model and to its politics: "local traditions" is the frank acknowledgment that some marks on the model were included because members of the model's audience expected them. Although written in the past tense, it should be in the present tense, like the rest of the text. In the half-century since its first presentation to the public, the model has continued to respond to its audiences' expectations. Those audiences have been dominantly Jewish and Christian; their expectations, though manifestly religious, are also deeply political.

For its Christian audience, the model is Herod's Jerusalem, the Jerusalem in which Jesus taught and worshipped and in which he was judged, condemned, executed, buried, and resurrected. Catholic visitors saw the site of those last two events marked both on the model and in the text of the pamphlet: "7. Traditional Calvary."[97] "Seven" marks the place (outside the walls, as in Amico's drawing) that has been occupied by the Church of the Holy Sepulchre since the fourth century. In the text, the claim of the site is identified as provisional by the use of the qualifying adjective, "traditional." On the model itself, the site of Calvary (Golgotha) was rendered as a dramatic outcrop with a spiral path to its top. Later, the place was reworked as an old quarry grown into a garden; at the foot of Calvary, an entrance into a cave-tomb was discernible. In its move to the Israel Museum, the site lost its topographic particularities and its garden-greenness. It is, consequently, much less visible. As many archaeologists recognize the legitimacy of the Holy Sepulchre as place marker for the historical location of the crucifixion and burial, its conditional status in the model now begs some explanation. Perhaps its provisionalness was a concession to the ever-increasing number of pious Protestant visitors, most of whom loath the hoary church. The overshadowing of the site of the

Church of the Holy Sepulchre appears to parallel the development of close political ties between Christian evangelical Zionism, the illegal settlement movement, and the Israeli right.[98]

The inconspicuousness of the site of the Holy Sepulchre allows evangelicals to witness a Jerusalem untainted by the detritus of idolatrous Catholics and Orthodox. Rather they find in the model's topography a prominent escarpment to the north of the city, identifying their alternative Calvary. That site, near Jeremiah's Grotto by the Damascus Gate, is known as Gordon's Tomb or the Garden Tomb. The first of those names derives from the site's popularizer, General Charles George Gordon, the famous British general, a pious evangelical Christian and martyr of Khartoum.[99] In the orthogonal lines of the topographical survey of Jerusalem by his fellow officer Colonel Sir Charles Warren, Gordon saw figured the body of the crucified Jesus in the landscape itself—the head was the new Golgotha with, nearby, an appropriately ancient rock-cut tomb.[100] The second name, now more common, describes the site's remaking by the Protestant Garden Tomb Association, UK, which bought the site in 1894, and continues to maintain it.[101] The locus, initially rather unsavory because of its proximity to Jerusalem's main abattoir, is now a lovely garden of the sort that Christians might imagine befitting the tomb of the wealthy Joseph of Arimathea. The association describes the setting without making scientific claims for its authenticity: "This Garden fits many of the details described in the gospel accounts. At the very least it is a beautiful visual aid that helps bring to life the wonderful events surrounding the Messiah's resurrection."[102] The site, which now no acknowledged archaeological authority identifies as the place of Jesus's burial and crucifixion, goes unremarked in all editions of the text accompanying the model. It is, however, marked on photographs of the model posted on websites appealing to Christian Zionists and reproduced in evangelical copies of the model, as in the Holy Land Experience theme park in Orlando.[103]

The most prominent audience for the model has always been Jewish. When the model was first opened, it served Jewish visitors not only as a scholarly archive, but also as a surrogate. The model provided a view of Jerusalem that was not otherwise available. Between the wars of 1948 and 1967, the whole of the Old City, including the

Kotel or Wailing Wall, the traditional focus of Jewish pilgrimage, was under Jordanian control and utterly inaccessible to Jews. The model provided a precious glimpse inside the Ottoman walls of a city that was otherwise hidden from view, a glimpse that confirmed the importance of Jerusalem and its Jewishness—Jerusalem without its Christian and Islamic accretions. Outside of the Ottoman walls and under the control of the Israelis was the southwest hill. This hill was misnamed Mount Zion after the construction of Herod's palace to its north; in the twelfth century "Mount Zion" was also misidentified as the location of the tomb of David.[104] That identify theft became particularly popular after 1948, when the "Tomb of David" substituted for the Wailing Wall as the primary focus of Jewish pilgrimage in Jerusalem.[105] The site's importance for national self-understanding trumped archaeological evidence for the model makers, as is acknowledged in its first explanatory pamphlet: "Near this palace [of Caiaphas] is a monument (25 on plan) which marks the site where the Tomb of David was believed to be from the time of the Second Temple onwards (the real tomb, then forgotten, was somewhere near 29 [Synagogue of the Freedmen] on the eastern hill.)"[106] The representation in the model of the tomb of David contradicts the archaeological record. It is a capitulation to the desires of the model's Jewish audience.

The shifts in the identity politics of the Jerusalem model are encoded in its naming. The title of the first guide to the model, published in 1966, was straightforward: "A Short Guide to the Model of Ancient Jerusalem." The current official title of the model—"Model of Jerusalem in the Second Temple Period"—is less so. The "Second Temple Period" is the modern name for an era that began in 538 BCE, when the Jews were freed from their Babylonian exile by the decree of the Persian king Cyrus. They returned to their province and subsequently rebuilt the first Temple, which had been destroyed by Nebuchadnezzar II. The end of the period is 70 CE, when Herod's new Temple was destroyed by the Romans during their suppression of the Jewish Revolt. For the innocent, the title wrongly suggests that the model's Temple represents the Persian-era second Temple of Jerusalem. Indeed, the awkward title of the model is conflated to "The Second Temple Jerusalem Model," in both academic and popular settings.[107] But there is no archaeological evidence that Herod's Temple complex, begun in 20/19 BCE and completed not long before its destruction, conformed to its predecessor. There is, however, documentary testimony to its difference.[108] "Model of Jerusalem in the Second Temple Period" appears, consequently, to be an elaborate way in which to avoid naming the Temple after the Roman-appointed Jewish convert, King Herod, who built it. Such a title obscures Palestine's historical condition at the turn of the first millennium—it was the Roman province of Judea. It enables even scholars to make problematic claims: "The Second Temple Model of Jerusalem . . . shows Jerusalem in the year 66 A.D. [sic], during the Second Temple period which represents national glory and cultural independence."[109]

The name change of the model, like the marks in its landscape, are subtle indices of its politics. Those political nuances of the modern analog model have been made more legible, at least to me, by the model's in-your-face use in the increasingly violent politics of Anthropocene Jerusalem. Now the model, translated into digital media, is used by right-wing, settler-supporting Jews and radical-right Christian-Zionist evangelicals to promote the construction of the Third Temple on the site of the Dome of the Rock (fig. 20). It is no longer a model of the past, but a model of the future Jerusalem, freed again from the debris of Muslims and deviant Christianities. The model makers' fervent commitment to historical authenticity was not enough to ensure the model's honest representation of the past. It certainly doesn't afford protection from the model's misappropriation of the future.

Simulacrum: Anthropocene Building Model

A final model of Jerusalem has both a very different form and a very different politics from its analog predecessor. This later model of the Holy City is accessible only digitally; it is found in a video game, *Assassin's Creed,* which was released by Ubisoft Montreal in 2007.[110] In the game, as the Assassin Altaïr Ibn-La'Ahad, I easily climb buildings and throw knives with deadly accuracy, things of which I am not capable in real life. But I move through medieval Jerusalem from the Church of the Holy Sepulchre to the Dome of the Rock in a way uncannily like

BIN EXCLUSIVE: SANHEDRIN ASKS PUTIN AND TRUMP TO BUILD THIRD TEMPLE IN JERUSALEM

By Adam Eliyahu Berkowitz November 10, 2016, 11:30 am

The Sanhedrin has requested that president-elect Donald Trump and Russian President Vladimir Putin work together to help rebuild the Temple. (Breaking Israel News)

FIG. 20. Adam Eliyahu Berkowitz, "Sanhedrin Asks Putin and Trump to Build Third Temple in Jerusalem." Latest News Biblical Perspective, *Breaking Israel News,* November 10, 2016. (Screen capture by the author)

I do modern Jerusalem—getting lost, bumping into shoppers, confronting and negotiating with a suspicious military that occupies both the streets and the rooftops (fig. 21). It is tricky to get into al-Haram al-Sharif (the Temple Mount), but even when I do, the Dome of the Rock is closed to me. As in Jerusalem now, the buildings of *Assassin's Creed's* Jerusalem are often more convincing than the humans and less confrontational.

There is also a correspondence between the game's politics and those of the actual world. *Assassin's Creed* is set in Syria-Palestine in the year 1191. King Richard the Lion-Hearted is the formidable leader of a Western invasion of the Holy Land confronting the land's astute defender, Salah ad-Din. There are both Christian and Muslim villains in the game—slavers, arms dealers, profiteers, book burners, corrupt governors—but those malefactors are all controlled by the Knights

Fig. 21. *Assassin's Creed*, 2009, Jerusalem, Altaïr at the Holy Sepulchre. (Screen capture by the author)

Templar. The Templars' broader agenda is to dominate the world by obtaining possession of magical "Pieces of Eden." Opposing their plot are the Assassins, represented by Altaïr. The English word "assassin" is derived from imaginative medieval accounts of the Hashashin, a heretical medieval Shi'a Muslim sect.[111] From the Middle Ages to the present, its members have been represented as expert killers for hire. The infamous daring of the Hashashin was ascribed to the manipulative use of hashish by their leader, the Old Man of the Mountain. Altaïr exacts information on the whereabouts of the "Pieces of Eden" from the Templar's evil sycophants before he eliminates them. Of the many first-person shooter video games set in the Crusades, *Assassin's Creed* is the only one I know in which the protagonist is a Muslim.

The Western gamer's Eastern ethnicity, imposed by the narrative, is reinforced by the game's forms. Its musical score tracks ethnic difference. Jesper Kyd's soundtrack for the game won the ELAN (Electronic Arts and Animation) award for the Best Video Game Soundtrack in 2008. As Kyd explains, each city in the game has its own musical character. "Acre is a Christian city with a western style instrumentation palette. . . . Here the musical tone is the most tragic because Acre endured a massive battle and is in ruins. Damascus is the proudest of the cities and a Muslim stronghold that had never been overtaken.

So the music here uses more traditional Middle Eastern arrangements from this time period and a slightly heroic tone."[112] The mood that the sound track produces is visually encoded in the models of the three principal cities in which action takes place. Damascus, a Muslim city, is golden—its hues are warm and its settings lavish. Its souk is well stocked; its structures are elaborate and beautifully ornamented. Its architectural centerpiece is the Great Mosque, rendered with a verisimilitude complete with opulent early eighth-century Byzantine mosaics. Minarets and domes create the city's filigree skyline. Acre, a Christian city, is rendered in desaturated blues. Smoking ruins and dead bodies pollute the city. Beggars are everywhere. The dominant motif of the distant view is the steeple: the great cathedral, with its unfinished facade, commands the jagged skyline. There are more beggars in Acre than elsewhere. Jerusalem, with its mixed Christian/Muslim population, is rendered greenishly, between the golds of Damascus and blues of Acre.

Assassin's Creed was produced by the French company Ubisoft in Canada during the bloody aftermath of George W. Bush's disastrous invasion of Iraq. Its narrative concentration on the elimination of warmongers as well as the unusual cultural partiality with which the game presents its Muslim sites and actors encodes the international community's horror at the consequences of Bush's war. The game's covert message is not that of Christian and Western triumphalism; it offers a subtle critique of neocolonial aggression. The model of Jerusalem in *Assassin's Creed* provides the compelling context for the game's action; it fully participates in the game's politics, both representing and enabling them. The models' political agency is programed into game. In contrast to the current politics of the Holy Land Hotel Model of Jerusalem, the model of Crusader Jerusalem always acted, more or less, as its producers intended. The models of the game perform politically, whether or not a gamer is conscious of their effects. And they rarely are. Altaïr is too busy assassinating targets and avoiding her own "desynchronization." Even video game critics and reviewers seem to have overlooked the macropolitical commentary of *Assassin's Creed*. It goes unmentioned in reviews.[113] The critiques of fascist power offered by *Assassin's Creed*'s sequels and spinoffs also go unnoticed. Critics panned 20th Century Fox's *Assassin's Creed*; none of them recognized its sotto voce condemnation of extremist religious movements now.[114]

The real-world politics of the Jerusalem model in *Assassin's Creed* are covert. As is so often the case now, the macropolitics of the world order are concealed by the micropolitics of global commerce. After all, a critique of American exceptionalism couldn't be too obvious if the game was to become, as it did, a blockbuster in the United States. Even the politics of the game's narrative are a diversion: they subvert Cartesian understandings of the clear distinction between good and bad. Freedom is not all that it's cracked up to be; control by a corporate elite has its benefits. The architectural models of the game, important agents in the construction of its ideological order, are also micropolitical diversions from its macropolitics. They are primary bearers of an exotic Middle Ages that distance the game experience from the world of the present. The models are seductively historical, though scientific correctness was not, as it was with the Holy Land Hotel Model, a priority. Nevertheless, the game makers' concern with their models' archaeological accuracy distinguishes *Assassin's Creed* within the genre of violent video games.[115] The digital rendering of the important monuments in Jerusalem is arresting, at least from the outside; the inside is forbidden. The Church of the Holy Sepulchre and the Dome of the Rock are impenetrable in *Assassin's Creed*. Perhaps they were closed because it was recognized that killing within them would be offensive to the religious sensibility of many of their players. Or perhaps they were inaccessible because of the large capital investment necessary to digitally construct those interiors.

Now interiors are accessible. *Assassin's Creed*'s many sequels—from ancient Egypt (*Assassin's Creed Origins*, 2017) and classical Athens (*Assassin's Creed Odyssey*, 2018) to the American and French Revolutions (*Assassin's Creed III*, 2012, and *Assassin's Creed Unity*, 2014)—not only manifest the ongoing popularity of the series, but also demonstrate the evolution of gaming technology. The Holy Sepulchre and the Dome of the Rock are closed in *Assassin's Creed*, but remarkably compelling models of complex medieval churches are open to sightseers in *Assassin's Creed*'s sequels. The best way for a student of Byzantine architecture to explore the interior of Hagia Sophia in Istanbul, especially now that the Great Church has been transformed from a museum into a mosque, is as the Assassin Ezio Auditore da Firenze in *Assassin's Creed Revelations* (2011; fig. 22). Experiencing the interior of Notre Dame in Paris as Arno Dorian in *Assassin's Creed Unity* (2014) is not so easy because the church is filled with my enemies, but it is still spectacular. It took Caroline Miousse, an artist at Ubisoft, fourteen months to research and create the model.[116] The PC version of the game was given away for free by Ubisoft after the shocking burning of Notre Dame in 2019.[117] Doubtless, there was a recognition of the economic benefit that might come from positive publicity and exposure, but the corporate gift also represented an empathetic response to a cultural catastrophe and the pride taken by a creative community in their product.

Technology moves on; it doesn't have a choice. Related to the inexorable development of computational technology is digital realism. High-end video games are increasingly filmic. Many treat video game realism as the cause or goad of technology's fecundity rather than its consequence. There is a widespread assumption that greater digital realism increases a model's persuasiveness. Video game designers strive to make their site of play so real that players have the illusion that their movement is unbounded. In his discussion of *Assassin's Creed*

FIG. 22. *Assassin's Creed,* Revelations, 2011, Istanbul. Ezio Auditore da Firenze at Hagia Sophia. (Screen capture by the author)

Revelations, Ubisoft's Michael Venables comments, "Naturally, it's impossible to create an exact replica of [Constantinople], but we have always managed to construct immersive environments that allow the player the *total freedom* to explore historically accurate and immense settings."[118] Gamers certainly engage with their games; in the grip of game play, heart rates increase.[119] But nonpsychotic gamers never become so entangled in the action that they believe that they or their avatars are "free." The world in which they act is always limited. Ezio can climb the great lunettes above the nave of Hagia Sophia, but he can't swim. A social scientific article makes the claim for the immersive potential of illusion with data sets to prove it: "The impact of graphical refinements . . . is not limited to improved esthetics—the increasing realism of video games has the additional effect of generating greater degrees of telepresence, defined as believable immersion within a mediated (e.g., virtual) environment."[120] This argument is made by researchers trained in marketing and "business intelligence." I have my doubts. Realism, as any art historian knows very well, can't be equated with "improved esthetics." More critically, while illusion is certainly seductive, the case for its equivalence with flow has yet to be convincingly proven. I was just as "immersed" in Spacewar! and Pong—which are famously abstract—when I first played them as I am now in *Assassin's Creed Odyssey.*[121]

It is the broad desire for new stimulus that drives the frenzy for hyperrealism; it is the profitable *promise* of an increasingly immersive gaming experience that promotes the development of illusionistic models for video games, not the actual delivery of greater flow. Computationally produced, ectypical spaces have long been fully immersive, though only in film and fiction (*Snow Crash* and *The Matrix*).[122] Although in an architect's office hyperreal digital models may be presented to clients as already in the world, digital models in video games have not yet morphed into habitable structures. Indeed, they tend to disappear altogether. At the time that it debuted, *Assassin's Creed*'s technology was cutting edge. In 2019, the game is no longer playable on current gaming platforms. I cannot revisit the Jerusalem of *Assassin's Creed* in the way that I might revisit the city of Jerusalem in Israel/Palestine or its analog model at the Israel Museum. But, as with the Buddhas of Bamiyan or the Temple of Bel in Palmyra to which I also cannot return, I remember my experience with representations: photographs and sketches from Syria and Afghanistan, snagged videos and screen shots from *Assassin's Creed*. I miss the Jerusalem of *Assassin's Creed*. Nostalgia is a neglected medium of video games. The disappearance of *Assassin's Creed's* Jerusalem is obviously the result of the corporation's fiscal decision making. Other games in the series have, after all, been remastered for marketing on new, more powerful platforms. There is always a politics involved in the decision to kill, even if the victim is only an economic good.

The problems involved in digital models colonizing the physical space of the world are addressed in the following chapter. I observe that as digital models come to structure human experience, they are certainly at least as political as the familiar analog models of the past. As with body models and medicine, the relationship between building models and architecture is intimately formative. Architectural change is inextricably tied to technological and conceptual shifts in model-making practices. How buildings look and act in the physical world depends on their models, and the forms of their models depend on the media and technologies by which those models are realized. More critically, different historical technologies of model making also embody different ways of spatializing the world—indexically, iconically, analogically, ectypically. The architectural model, like all models, is certainly historical. It is also, like all models, political, as I hope this chapter has demonstrated.

4
Black Boxes

> The total reality is the world.
> We make to ourselves pictures of facts.
> The picture presents the facts in logical space, the existence and non-existence of atomic facts.
> The picture is a model of reality.
>
> —Ludwig Wittgenstein, *Tractatus Logico-Philosophicus*

Boxes

Boxes, closed and secretive, are seductive. Elaborate puzzle boxes and ornamental jewelry cases arouse desire for what is inside. Even an Amazon delivery box is magical: hidden anonymously in neat, brown symmetry, the commodity within escapes its banality until it is revealed. If "box" derives circuitously from the Greek "pyxis," as the *Oxford English Dictionary* cautiously suggests, its acts of enclosure involve artifice. Pyxides are small containers, often made of luxury materials and elaborately decorated. Their embellishment is a sign of the preciousness of their contents. They were made in antiquity for costly unguents, jewels, and medicinal preparations. In the Christian Middle Ages, they also held relics and eucharistic wafers. Like all boxes, a pyxis might confine as well as protect its contents. Emblematic of all such small prisons is Pandora's pyxis. Pandora, the first woman, was made by Zeus to punish Prometheus and all men for the theft of fire from the gods. In accounts of the incident by Hesiod and later Greek authors, Zeus gives a wedding gift to Pandora and Epimetheus, Prometheus's brother and the gullible human husband who accepted her as his wife. The gift was a *pithos,* not to be unsealed. Human curiosity leads to its opening; the evils entrapped inside escape to make the hitherto idyllic world miserable.[1] *Pithos* is the Greek word for the sort of very large clay jar that was used in antiquity for storage, shipping, and burial.[2] Early modern Latin versions of the Greek story of Pandora identify the offending vessel not as a *dolium* (a large jar, the Latin equivalent of *pithos*), but as a *pyxis* (small box). This change from a big earthen receptacle into a diminutive, ornamental box has been ascribed to the great humanist and intellectual Erasmus, and identified as a "philological accident."[3] I might suggest that Erasmus's translation was less an accident than an exercise of artistic license. Erasmus uses Pandora's story to illustrate the adage "Hostium munera non munera" or "Enemies' gifts are not gifts."[4] A beautiful box is, after all, a more seductive gift than a storage jug. Now the word "pyxis" rarely occurs outside of a museum catalogue. There it describes an ancient, highly wrought container emptied of its contents and incarcerated as art in an institutional vitrine.

The Anthropocene version of Pandora's pyxis is the black box. This black box is not the indestructible recording device so familiar from news reports after airline disasters. That box is designed to be opened to reveal that which cannot otherwise be known; its contents are complex, but comprehensible. Rather, it is the other, much more ubiquitous black box, into which seeing is impossible. The operator of this kind of black box controls its input and uses its output, but doesn't question the means by which the data that is entered is transformed into the result that emerges. The source of the term "black box" is myth presented as history. Like Pandora's box, the black box is understood to have originated in man's struggle with evil. In the 1940s, new radar technology that might determine the outcome of the war against fascism was discovered by British researchers. This technology had to be developed and manufactured in the United States because of desperate materiel shortages in Great Britain. It was clandestinely transported across the Atlantic in a black metal box. That box gave its name to impenetrable boxes that held powerful secrets.[5] Whatever its inception, by the 1950s "black box" had infiltrated the rhetoric of a variety of sciences and social sciences, from the behavioral to the computational. "To the student of behavior, the animal is the proverbial 'black box.' By manipulating its inputs and observing its outputs, he attempts to arrive at generalizations regarding the mechanism within."[6] "Experimental psychology has lately come to concern itself more and more with the human being as a 'black box', having certain characteristic ways of receiving and reacting to information."[7] "The most distinctive electronic block or element in the NORC [IBM's Naval Ordnance Research Calculator] is the Dynamic Pulse circuit. This is a small assembly of vacuum tubes, resistors, capacitors and diodes, which operates as a unit. This element can be thought of logically as a 'little black box' having an input terminal and an output terminal, each of which can be attached to a signal line of the machine."[8]

In 1963, Mario Bunge, a physicist and philosopher of science, offered an algorithmic model of this black box:

$$R(t) = \int_{-\infty}^{t} du\, M(t, u) F[S(u - \tau)]$$

He explained his alphanumeric model: "A black box is a fiction representing a set of concrete systems into which stimuli S impinge and out of which reactions R emerge. The constitution and structure of the box are altogether irrelevant to the approach under consideration, which is purely external or phenomenological. In other words, only the behavior of the system will be accounted for. . . . [T]he box itself is regarded as a unit rather than a system of interdependent parts."[9] What goes on within a black box is irrelevant; what goes into the box and what comes out is all that matters. A "black box" encloses operations that have an effect, but which are themselves a mystery.

The black box might well have been a "fiction" in the 1960s, as Bunge described it. But now the black box more commonly acts as a metaphor.[10] Certainly, I am beset by metaphorical black boxes. My life is filled with things that execute tasks by means beyond my comprehension. My computer, upon which I am utterly dependent, seems often not to need me at all. It continually miscorrects my punctuation and updates itself without my conscious permission. My automobile answers my cell phone and tells me when to put on its brakes. My toothbrush makes a smiley face at me when I properly clean my molars. I can't figure out how to make my Bluetooth device act like an old-fashioned radio and turn on to NPR. When any of these many inscrutable things fails to function, I have no idea how to fix it. The "black box" in my account is a very *flabby* metaphor—it applies loosely and personally to objects that are closed to me, but which might be opened and easily understood by more technologically competent humans. Metaphorical black boxes, particularly those of the flabby variety, proliferate exponentially in the twenty-first century. They may be hazardous to your health as well as to your self-esteem. Good health, after all, is not just a matter of physical well-being; good health also implies a mental awareness of the self's limitations and the ability to accommodate to them. Good health is a vulnerable thing.[11]

Metaphorical black boxes are particularly threatening to good health when they usurp models. Models necessarily falsify some aspects of their referents. They are, nevertheless, remarkably helpful in getting to the truth of the world so long as the parameters of their prevarication are understood. When black boxes appropriate models, however, model makers and model users lose track not only of their models' limitations but also of their own. Flabbily metaphoric black boxes make socially abhorrent cityscapes. When those black boxes become muscular metaphors, they are even more dangerous. They make pandemic impugners and climate change deniers.

Flabby Metaphors

BIM (building information modeling) is an example of a flabbily metaphoric black box. BIM was begotten of CAD (computer-aided design); it names computer programs that produce four-dimensional models—three-dimensional renderings with an added layer saturated with data. These programs manipulate modular components, generating the broad scaffold of a project along with all of its particulars. BIM allows multiple collaborators (developers, architects, engineers, contractors, clients) to coproduce an interactive digital model by means of a shared software that is connected with big data (architectural elements, market prices, wind velocities, and the like). BIM allows users to visualize in different graphic registers (planer, three-dimensional, hyperreal) the physical components of a building (structural, plumbing, and electrical systems), its programmatic features (function and circulation), and its aesthetic attributes (furnishings, finishes, artwork, lighting effects).[12] BIM programs can provide the current costs of particular configurations. They enable the identification of financial and other efficiencies not only during construction, but also for future building operation. BIM promises all that is pragmatically knowable about its object for those who design, build, manage, and inhabit it, as well as for those who profit from it. The reach of BIM is extended by computational prosthetics. Complemented by GIS (geography information system), it documents a project's relation to its physical environment. Experienced in VR (virtual reality), it allows stakeholders to investigate the structure before its material realization.[13] In architecture, BIM is used for heritage projects (HBIM) as well as new builds.[14] All major institutions, private and public, now have BIM protocols for construction. BIM has permanently evicted the drafting board from the architectural studio; it has displaced sketchbooks and basswood in the conceptual work of space making.[15]

Computer-aided design has, of course, lots to offer. It has enabled starchitects to produce playful and powerful monuments, like Frank Gehry's Guggenheim Museum in Bilbao and Zaha Hadid's Heydar Aliyev Center in Baku, Azerbaijan. And it promises digital mass customization.[16] BIM's greatest advantages are more practical: nonredundancy, communication efficiency, and cost-effectiveness.[17] BIM and its computational sequels are here to stay. But, like all powerful systems, BIM also has its dangers.[18] Perhaps most notoriously, it is duplicitously seductive. BIM produces a compellingly finished-looking object while that object is still very much a work in progress. Naive architects and contractors as well as naive clients may be deluded into mistaking as complete an incomplete project. Less obviously but perhaps even more insidiously, BIM's modularity provides its users with the formidable ability of deploying a model designed for one location to another. The design of the first model might well be managed by a competent architect. By a competent architect, I mean an architect who has an experienced understanding of materials, scale, and circulation; she carefully balances the multiple factors involved in making a good building (physical, aesthetic, social, financial). For her, the BIM program is not a black box—she rewrites the code to modify it when it is recalcitrant. But when BIM is deployed by operators who can't write the code necessary to control it—that is, for those users for whom BIM is a black box—BIM's progeny may be monstrous. Moreover, a model, whether good or bad, can readily be used abominably by those who privilege only one of the factors of architecture—namely its profitability. For developers whose only real interest in construction is profit, BIM is a most useful black box. For those who endure its spawn in the landscape, BIM is an invidious one.

The infestation in American cities by grotesque, block-eating, medium-rise, "luxury" apartment buildings is evidence of that invidiousness (fig. 23). These massive structures are ugly; their uncontrolled multiplication makes them hideous. They take the form of enormous parti-colored, volume-less boxes. Their relentless scale is masked with bump-out bays, faux-brick sections, and neutral cladding panels interspaced with brightly colored ones—metal on the facade, vinyl in the back. Corner features may be capped with Italianate projecting eaves *sans* corbels or low-pitched roofs. Walls are occasionally crowned with pseudo-cornices. They flatten a filigree skyline with billboard banality. Their construction explains their impression as mere surface: a two-story concrete base supports a five-story, stick-frame superstructure

FIG. 23. Durham Gateway Apartments, Durham, North Carolina, April 2020. (Photograph by the author)

often wrapped around a multideck concrete carpark. They are all alike. These structures are designed not by the same architect, but by the same algorithm.

The blight is not just aesthetic. Those who live in these massive agglomerations of rental units suffer, as do those who have to look at them. These complexes offer social amenity spaces which act as lures: swimming pools, exercise rooms, lounges, pool tables, dog parks. With the exception of the dog park, these social spaces are almost always empty. The dog park is popular as a frame for the mating rituals of humans as well as animals; it also affords protection to those who might otherwise have to encounter real urban space. The transient millennials who populate these structures don't look up from their cell phones when they pass their fellow residents in the endless windowless hallways by which they circulate within them. Anyone over forty is utterly invisible. Those on early-morning schedules occasionally encounter the vomit left behind the night before by another inmate. The noncommunity that occupies the site imposes its self-indulgent introversion on its surroundings. Amazon Prime makes local retail unnecessary; Grub Hub means that nearby restaurants lose more customers than they gain because parking inconveniences are aggravated by the block's visitors. These parasitical complexes promote gentrification at the same time that they eliminate the potential of city neighborhoods. They are nonplaces—an expression of suburban sprawl come back to haunt urban life.[19]

Nonplaces are usually the products of property developers working with BIM in collusion with zoning ordinances, building codes, banks, and REITs (real estate investment trusts). BIM pretends to allow the architect the freedom to invent a building. But, of course, freedom is as much of an illusion in architectural offices as it is in video games. Unlike gamers who recognize the programmatic limitations on their play, some architects seem sometimes to forget that they are not free. Unless they can modify code, they are as controlled by their programs as any avatar. The making of buildings on their screens is certainly facilitated by their programs, but it is also restricted. What might seem the product of an architect's spatial imagination may be the creation of a BIM program put together by techies who are utterly indifferent to the built landscape. After all, the founders of Autodesk, the industry-dominant corporation, developed AutoCAD out of a concern for their share of the emerging industry, not out of any interest in architecture. Now that they have a stranglehold on the market, they are notoriously unwilling to invest their enormous profits in making their BIM platform, Revit, better.[20] To the naive architect, the computer screen's interface may appear transparent; the field that the screen presents may seem like free space, liberated from restraints of T-squares and compasses, of scale and weight, of Mylar and rapidographs. The object produced on the screen is no longer an assemblage of predesigned modules for a yet-to-be-realized physical object. That is, for the naive designer, the entity on the screen is not a model but, rather, it is the real thing. The black box tricks architects and their patrons into forgetting that the photo-realistic image produced on their screens and websites does not already exist materially in the world. In a manner that would have surprised even Alberti, the architect's image has become the building; the physical structure in the landscape is a mere copy.[21]

Muscular Metaphors

The true mettle of the black box as a metaphor was tested by Bruno Latour in his *Laboratory Life* (1979) and later more fully demonstrated in his *Science in Action* (1987). In both texts, "black box" is a muscular metaphor deployed to restrain the then reigning authority of science. Latour identifies progress in science as a "game," but he characterizes it more like a war. "Scientific activity is not 'about nature,' it is a fierce fight to construct reality."[22] Each skirmish is a claim about some aspect of the world. A claim, highly researched and meticulously demonstrated, wins its battle by gaining broad acceptance among other investigators. Once victorious, the claim is incorporated into the accepted truth of science and is no longer subject to interrogation. Latour describes such unchallenged claims as black boxes. Their credibility is economic as well as intellectual: it is too costly to rework those old formulas on which new ones are already based.[23] These black-boxed claims, he insists, need to be reopened and understood for what they are: the products of particular times, of various political and financial forces, of distinct interests.[24] In the late twentieth century, Latour could still legitimately assume that black boxes were metaphors for closed objects that might yet be pried open to reveal their contents. In the early twenty-first century, some black boxes are permanently sealed. "Black box" might still be a metaphor; after all, a model disappears into a dark, hermetically sealed encasement only figuratively, not literally. But that metaphor is now a very muscular one. The most ominous of these black boxes are ones that predict the future.

Prediction is the modern form of prophecy. Neither prophecy nor prediction concerns banal, repetitive phenomena—taxes, tides, death. Both address anxieties about dangerous uncertainties—how much taxes and tides will rise or when death will occur. Prophecy, whispered to humans by the gods, comes true. Moses knew about the plagues of Egypt prior to their occurrence; Noah knew about the flood before it happened. Predictions, in contrast to prophecies, are never absolutely certain, only statistically probable.[25] Even those predictions made by known and trusted sources about relatively stable phenomena are not always reliable, as the U.S. election of 2016 demonstrated. Models have long been deployed in prediction making—from building schemes to orreries. At present, models are habitually part of the process of prediction, though they are usually forgotten unless a prediction turns out to be wrong. In the early stages of the COVID-19 pandemic, governmental decisions that delayed shutdowns and the acquisition of medical supplies in many countries resulted in tens of thousands of deaths. Some of those politicians' choices have been blamed on mathematical models, though the ideological dimension of the politicians' actions seems clear enough to most of us.[26] Models have become an easy scapegoat because of their inaccessibility. So long as it was understood how models were made and how they worked, their limitations were detectable and their predictions appraisable. Difficulties arise when the phenomena being modeled and the models themselves have become impenetrably complex. Weather models are a perfect example.[27]

Weather has always affected humans, and humans have habitually attempted to control those effects. Contending with extreme weather has taken a variety of forms. There are always those who believe that it can be manipulated through incantation and prayer. In the Chapel of Queen Elizabeth I, in 1559, drought elicited a prayer for its end:

> For fair weather. O Lord God, which for the sin of man didst once drown all the world except eight persons, and afterward of thy great mercy didst promise never to destroy it so again: we humbly beseech thee, that although we for our iniquities have worthily deserved this plague of rain and waters; yet upon our true repentance thou wilt send us such weather, whereby we may receive the fruits of the earth in due season, and learn both by thy punishment to amend our lives, and for thy clemency to give thee praise and glory, through Jesus Christ our Lord. Amen.[28]

General George S. Patton famously had a similar prayer read by his troops at Christmas time in 1944 to facilitate his defeat of the Germans.[29] Bad weather in the twenty-first century continues to elicit such invocations.[30]

The rational study of the atmosphere offered the means of understanding weather and preparing for its effects, if not of controlling it. Natural philosophy was one of the more powerful of these mechanisms.[31] From Aristotle to Descartes, weather was explained in terms of the natural order of the physical world.

> There are two kinds of exhalation, moist and dry, and the atmosphere contains them both potentially. It, as we have said before, condenses into cloud, and the density of the clouds is highest at their upper limit. (For they must be denser and colder on the side where the heat escapes to the upper region and leaves them. This explains why hurricanes and thunderbolts and all analogous phenomena move downwards in spite of the fact that everything hot has a natural tendency upwards. Just as the pips that we squeeze between our fingers are heavy but often jump upwards: so these things are necessarily squeezed out away from the densest part of the cloud.)[32]

Anecdotal observation of nature and logic anchor Aristotle's argument. There is no need for the gods' intervention.

In modernity, natural philosophy, if not the divine will, was superseded by science as the preferred means of getting a grip on the weather. Science depends on the collection of empirical data and its rational interpretation. Instruments were developed to measure weather phenomena in antiquity and the Middle Ages (wind direction, rainfall, and humidity) and in early modernity (more sophisticated hygrometers, barometers, and thermometers).[33] The predictive capacity of such measurements was, however, seriously limited by their spatial isolation. Forecasting only became possible after the invention and widespread deployment of the telegraph offered a means of rapidly gathering weather data from across an extended territory. Refinements in weather prediction and war were interdependent, as is the case with so many new technologies. In the 1870s, in the United States, for example, the military's interest in weather prediction led to a confrontation between Western Union, which held a virtual monopoly on telegraphic communication, and the federal government.[34] In the twentieth century, Lewis Fry Richardson made the earliest attempt to mathematize weather forecasting in the trenches of World War I.[35] After the war, in the early 1920s, Richardson envisioned a most remarkable model for weather prediction—the "forecast factory."

> Imagine a large hall like a theatre, except that the circles and galleries go right round through the space usually occupied by the stage. The walls of this chamber are painted to form a map of the globe. The ceiling represents the north polar regions, England is in the gallery, the tropics in the upper circle, Australia on the dress circle and the Antarctic in the pit. A myriad of computers are at work upon the weather of the part of the map where each sits, but each computer attends only to one equation or part of an equation. The work of each region is coordinated by an official of higher rank. . . . From the floor of the pit a tall pillar rises to half the height of the hall. It carries a large pulpit on its top. In this sits the man in charge of the whole theatre; he is surrounded by several assistants and messengers. . . . But instead of waving a baton he turns a beam of rosy light upon any region that is running ahead of the rest, and a beam of blue light upon those who are behindhand. Four senior clerks in the central pulpit

are collecting the future weather as fast as it is being computed, and dispatching it by pneumatic carrier to a quiet room. There it will be coded and telephoned to the radio transmitting station. . . . Outside are playing fields, houses, mountains and lakes, for it was thought that those who compute the weather should breathe of it freely.[36]

Stephen Conlin offers an amusing illustration of this panoptic-like theater model full of human computers (fig. 24).

Nonhuman computers met the extensive numerical demands of relatively simple weather system models only in the 1960s. Now there are many complex programs producing weather system models. The "spaghetti" maps of the predicted paths of hurricanes are perhaps the most familiar representations of the various weather prediction

FIG. 24. "Weather Forecasting Factory" by Stephen Conlin, based on the description in "Weather Prediction by Numerical Process" by L. F. Richardson, Cambridge University Press, 1922, and on advice from Prof. John Byrne, Trinity College Dublin. (Image: ink and watercolour © Stephen Conlin 1986, All Rights Reserved)

models available to forecasters. The most reliable predictions come from the European Centre for Medium-Range Weather Forecasts (ECMWF), an independent intergovernmental organization supported by thirty-four European nations, including Turkey, with cooperating states also from the Middle East and North Africa.[37] As its name suggests, the ECMWF specializes in medium-range weather forecasts (ten to fifteen days into the future) though they also offer long-range forecasts (up to forty days into the future). Weather forecasting is about the changing atmospheric conditions in the present and near future. Describing broader shifts in the earth's climate is a very different matter.

"Climate" is used to describe average conditions over a thirty-year period; predicting changes in the climate involves the next generation of humans. Judging from nineteenth- and early twentieth-century articles in *Scientific American*, early investigations of climate change tended to find that there was no such thing.[38] When change in the climate was acknowledged, its explanation was often mechanical. Ludwig Staby, for example, ascribed climate change to the oscillation of the earth's axis. "Hitherto the causation of the successive geological periods, including the glacial periods, through which the earth has passed, has remained an inexplicable mystery, but this mystery becomes as clear as day in the light of the pendulation theory."[39] In the late twentieth and early twenty-first century, with the exponentially expanded capacity to gather, mathematize, and model data, doubt about climate change has all but disappeared within the scientific community. There is consensus now among the experts. Of the credentialed scientists working in the field, 97 percent subscribe to anthropogenic—human-induced—global warming.[40] Further, most of the leading scientific organizations worldwide have issued public statements endorsing this position.[41]

As we are all too well aware, those scientists have not yet (in 2021) succeeded in convincing corporate CEOs in the fossil fuel industry, rabid evangelical preachers, or my Republican brother that the problem of anthropogenic global warming is serious enough to cut into profits or to acknowledge reason. In consequence, the policy makers who depend on the political support of those unconvinced constituencies take no action. What is responsible for this lack of persuadability?

At least in part, climate change models. For those who make and decipher them, these models consistently demonstrate that the earth is warming and that humans have contributed to that increasingly catastrophic condition. The problem is that to just about everyone else these same models are utterly opaque. The data being modeled (atmospheric aerosols, carbon cycle representations, chemical volatilities) are increasing, as is the number of scientists, institutions, and technicians involved in the models' construction. Multiple models are necessary to ensure predictive possibility.[42] Nevertheless, climate-modeling programs are now so many and diverse that there are models of how to select the best models for particular climatological questions.[43] As Gavin Schmidt, director of the NASA Goddard Institute for Space Studies, noted over a decade ago: "Today's models are flexible tools that can answer a wide range of questions, but at a price: They can be almost as difficult to analyze and understand as the real world."[44]

Those who for venal reasons oppose attempts to reduce carbon omissions commonly base their denunciations on the impenetrability of climate change models. Typically simplistic arguments against anthropogenic climate change offered by Kerry Jackson and Patrick Michaels (agent of the Cato Institute, the Koch brothers' libertarian think tank, which in the past worked for the tobacco industry, arguing that smoking is not unhealthy), reveal how a broad misunderstanding of models allows utterly vacuous contentions to appear reasonable.

> The global warming alarmists tell us to trust the science. But when it comes to climate studies, there's less science and more accounting going on there. Computer models have an important place in science. They are useful in helping us understand our world, but models themselves aren't science. *Encyclopaedia Britannica* says "scientific models at best are approximations of the objects and systems that they represent," but "they are not exact replicas." In the case of climate models, they are not even close to being approximate replicas.[45]

Like all models, climate change models are not True. Suggesting that models are not science is like claiming that reason and logic are not science—science cannot be done without them. Or again:

BLACK BOXES   115

To summarize [this Google Scholar search], it looks like something like 55% of the modeling done in all of science is done in climate change science, even though it is a tiny fraction of the whole of science. Moreover, within climate change science almost all the research (97%) refers to modeling in some way.... Climate science appears to be obsessively focused on modeling. Modeling can be a useful tool, a way of playing with hypotheses to explore their implications or test them against observations. That is how modeling is used in most sciences. But in climate change science modeling appears to have become an end in itself. In fact, it seems to have become virtually the sole point of the research.... Climate change research should be focused on improving our understanding, not modeling from ignorance.[46]

By means of Google Scholar searches, the authors determine that climate change research is dominated by models. (It might be noted that the same method suggests, for example, that 71 percent of Cato Institute economics is model-dependent.) Basing a "scientific" argument on raw numbers drawn from Google searches may just be naive, but the authors' description of models and their role in science is, by Harry Frankfurt's definition, "bullshit."[47] A more serious critique of the role of models in the climate change debate is offered by the well-known climatologist Mike Hulme, who argues that models assert too much authority.[48] But I don't expect that Hulme would endorse the notion that a model is simply a toy for "playing with hypotheses," as Michaels alleges. Models make hypotheses more robust.[49]

Of course, climate change models have their limits.[50] As early as 1987, Stephen H. Schneider, professor of environmental biology and global change at Stanford University, provided an appropriate analogy for our understanding of climate models:

> Climate models do not yield definitive forecasts of what the future will bring; they provide only a dirty crystal ball in which a range of plausible fortunes can be glimpsed. They thereby pose a dilemma: we are forced to decide how long to keep cleaning the glass before acting on what we think we see inside . . . ? At present, we are altering our environment faster than we can understand the resulting climatic

changes. If the trend does not stop, we shall eventually either verify or disprove the climate models—by means of a real, global experiment whose consequences we shall not escape.[51]

The climate crisis of the present cannot be blamed on models. Climate change models only act according to their nature. They can't convey the whole truth; they only help us get into truth's closer proximity. Nor can they be expected to be convincing to those who aren't familiar with their hermeneutic conventions. Finally, how they are able to act is moderated. Those who know and love them attempt to interpret their predictions for us; they appeal to our reasonableness and our commitment to the futures of our grandchildren. Some do that job better than others.[52]

Models and Discourse

The debates in the first decades of the twenty-first century over climate change models are evidence of models' dependence on discourse. Climate change models demonstrate that the effectiveness of a model may well rely on the effectiveness with which it is explained. Indeed, many models depend on texts to exercise their agency. An economic pie chart that has no labels or no accompanying account is useless. Without a text, an innocent viewer might think that a beautiful arrangement of glass balls was a delicate sculpture rather than a model of cyclohexane, methane, ethane, and heptane molecules (fig. 25).

Models stand in a variety of relationships to texts. There are models that are so much like texts that they might be taken to be texts—for example, algorithms. Other models might be imbedded in texts. Henry David Thoreau's *Walden*, for example, might well function as a model.[53] We understand the assignment when a high school teacher directs her students: "Spend one hour alone closely observing nature. Draft an informal essay or response, modeled on *Walden*, to describe your thoughts and feelings."[54] Similarly, *Walden* is taken as a model, if somewhat vaguely, by B. F. Skinner for the fictional community in his novel, *Walden Two*.[55] There, a text acts as a model for another text. Of course, to function as a model, the relevant bits of *Walden* must be

Fig. 25. 3D glass molecular model created by Purpy Pupple, November 22, 2010. (Purpy Pupple—own work, CC BY-SA 3.0, *https://commons.wikimedia.org/w/index.php?curid=12121577*)

removed from the source and reconstructed analogically or abstractly as a model. That process of extrapolating a model from the text is its making. It might be argued that, though the model is dependent on a text, it is itself not a text, but rather a formula, a diagram, an idea. Although some texts may be identified as models, models should not be mistaken for texts.[56]

Other models eschew texts altogether; their meaning can be adequately grasped without the help of a text. The model by which bees negotiate a terrain has nothing whatsoever to do with words; rather a bee's metric map is derived from familiar topography.[57] Understanding a supermodel like Naomi Campbell certainly depends on a familiarity with her cultural context, but it does not rely on an explanatory written description. A child does not require a manual in order to play with a doll's house.[58]

Not all models are engaged in textual relations, but all models are involved in discourse. For the *Oxford English Dictionary*, "discourse" is still exclusively about language: "The body of statements, analysis, opinions, etc., relating to a particular domain of intellectual or social activity, especially as characterized by recurring themes, concepts, or values; also the set of shared beliefs, values, etc., implied or expressed by this." For those of us in the humanities, however, discourse has expanded to include, in addition to linguistic forms, nonverbal things and practices—uniforms, airport security, table settings, media platforms—that articulate and enable the exercise of power relationships. Michel Foucault expanded the scope of discourse by persuasively describing the participation of vision and the body in the emergent modern state's new and effective forms of discipline.[59] In the sciences and social sciences, models have become a dominant means of articulating problems, representing theories, and offering descriptions of the world. The scientific model's complex interactions with its makers, observers, and referents in the world are negotiated through a wide variety of recognized media, from robotic data collection to scholarly articles. Scientific discourse is committedly conventionalized. Its quantitative values and qualitative expressions are ordered by broadly accepted symbolic forms and institutional hierarchies. Climate change models are possible not only because of the proliferation of data collection stations in the world but also because of the standardization of the data that is collected. Whose climate change models are taken most seriously depends on the reputation of the scientists who produce them and the prestige of the institutions that support the research involved in their making. In the arts, the humanities, and daily life, the model's modes of mediation tend to be less formal. The nonscientific model relates with ease and intimacy to its human producers and consumers through a less ordered, but equally complex web of texts, narratives, images, objects, and habits. The model's capacity to produce stories as well as to illustrate them derives, at least in part, from its singularity.

Models, whether in the form of the medieval diagram, the early modern icon, the modern analog, or the Anthropocene simulacrum, have always depended on their material and linguistic contexts to give them meaning and make them effective. To provide good explanations, good models require good explainers, something that too often goes unremarked in discussion.[60] As pandemic and climate change models suggest, some Anthropocene models, especially those emerging from black boxes, may need a more elaborate critical apparatus than those of premodernity and modernity. Better means of effectively conveying the lessons that models teach us must be found. Now our lives depend upon it.

The final definition summarizes the argument of this book:

> A model is an autonomous agent that has a referent (material, ideal, conceptual, imaginary, . . .) to which it adverts (mimetically, symbolically, symptomatically, inferentially, . . .), but from which it differs in significant ways (in its complexity, scale, material, function, way of being-in-the-world, . . .). In its relation to its referent, a model is weak or strong, sometimes oscillating between the two. A model assumes its interpreter's familiarity with its particular hermeneutic conventions. Although no model can ever licitly make truth claims, a model can be good or bad, honest or dishonest. A good model is an epistemic operator that works (abstractly, critically, ludically . . .) toward a fuller understanding of the world. All models have histories. All models act politically. And all models are entangled in discourse.

NOTES

Introduction

1. Most recently, Brueckner, Isenstadt, and Wasserman, *Modelwork*, and *Model Behavior*, a special issue of *Log*.
2. Black, *Models and Metaphors*; Wartofsky, *Models*; Wendler, *Das Modell zwischen Kunst und Wissenschaft*; Magnani and Bertolotti, *Springer Handbook of Model-Based Science*.
3. Morgan, *The World in the Model*, 176–212.
4. For an accessible if polemical historiography of periodization, see Le Goff, *Must We Divide History into Periods?*
5. For a classic critique of the modern, see Latour, *We Have Never Been Modern*.
6. Jameson, *Postmodernism*; Hayles, *How We Became Posthuman*.
7. Crutzen, "Geology of Mankind"; Davies, *The Birth of the Anthropocene*; Fagan, "On the Dangers of an Anthropocene Epoch."

1. Unmanageable Models/Definition

1. Goodman, *Languages of Art*, 171.
2. Michael Krämer, a theoretical particle physicist, suggests that the new complexity of data and its processing will not only modify models, but also philosophy: "The Philosophy of the Large Hadron Collider." For the changed effects of models and their greater prominence with the development of big data, see, for example, Morrison, *Reconstructing Reality*, and Basso, Lisciandra, and Marchionni, "Hypothetical Models in Social Science."
3. Other short definitions of "model" have been offered. See for example, Arata, "A Unified View of Models," 282. He posits that a model is "an interface that enables the performance of tasks according to preferences," though this definition denies a model its own life. Even shorter: "A possible realization in which all valid sentences of a theory T are satisfied is called a model of T"; Tarski, "A General Method in Proofs of Undecidability," 11. Ronald Giere, who understands models as "the primary (though by

no means the only) representational tools in the sciences," offers perhaps the most succinct definition: S [scientist] uses X [model] to represent W [world] for purposes P; Giere, "How Models Are Used to Represent Reality," 746–47.

4. In the sciences, a model's referent is commonly referred to as a "target." Target, however, implies a misleading unidirectionality.

5. Wartofsky, *Models*, 4.

6. Charles Peirce's familiar observations on the means by which things signify as signs offer a convenient shorthand for the wide spectrum of linkages between a model and its referent—icon, index, and symbol. Peirce defined these terms in several different texts, one of which is Peirce, *Collected Papers*, 2.156–73. For an overview, see Atkin. "Peirce's Theory of Signs."

7. Or by deduction, induction, or abduction—in the Peircian sense of an understanding derived from limited evidence and informed conjecture.

8. The master of the social index is Bourdieu, *Distinction*.

9. Jordanova, "Material Models as Visual Culture," 447.

10. For a useful overview of various current understandings of the ontology of the scientific model, see Gelfert, "The Ontology of Models."

11. "Delray Arms Company Reportedly Linked to Gun in Paris Attack," CBS Miami, 2015. http://miami.cbslocal.com/2015/12/11/delray-arms-company-reportedly-linked-to-gun-in-paris-attack-issues-statement/.

12. The discussion of these terms is dependent on definitions given in the Oxford English Dictionary.

13. Johnson, *Notes to Shakespeare*, 3.1.161 (239, 2).

14. Dee, "Preface," ciij v.

15. For a definition of an isomorphic model, see Baget et al., "On Rules with Existential Variables," 1648. For what seems to be a clear definition of model theory (universal algebra + logic = model theory), see, Chang and Keisler, *Model Theory*, 1. For a stimulating definition of mathematical models which, however, understands models as marginal to the production of knowledge, see Badiou, *The Concept of the Model*, esp. 12–13.

16. Ferri, "The Curse of the Yale Model." I am indebted to Jessica Newman who wrote a fine paper on this subject for my "Models" seminar at Duke in spring 2015.

17. Buono, "Models of Central Pattern Generators for Quadruped Locomotion."

18. "Strong" and "weak" are terms sometimes used in relation to a model's predictive success. E.g., Collyer, "Notes and Comment." The prognostic

accuracy of models is discussed below in terms of their epistemological performance.
19. Geertz, "Religion as a Cultural System," 93. On "model of" and "model for" also see McCarty, "Modeling."
20. Brown, "Thing Theory," 4.
21. In Morgan and Morrison, *Models as Mediators*, chap. 3. For a brilliant analysis of economic models and their histories, also see Morgan, *The World in the Model*.
22. Gelfert, *How to Do Science with Models*, vi.
23. Latour, *Reassembling the Social*.
24. Wharton. *Architectural Agents*. I have also defined agency elsewhere, for example, see Wharton, "Scaffold, Model, Metaphor."
25. Anderson, *A Dictionary of Law*. For a more modern, more detailed, but less cogent legal definition of "agent," see Law and Martin. "A Dictionary of Law."
26. Trudeau and Levinthal, *Hitler Moves East*.
27. For a good introduction to scientific representation and models as fictions, see Taylor, "*Information and Scientific Representation.*"
28. Popper, *The Myth of the Framework*, 172–73.
29. Badiou, *The Concept of the Model*, 15–16. Badiou's italics.
30. Levins, "The Strategy of Model Building in Population Biology," 431. Levins also aptly describes what must be sacrificed in models: generality to realism and precision, realism to generality and precision, precision to realism and generality (422).
31. Casti, *Alternate Realities*, 458.
32. Peschard, "Forging Model/World Relations: Relevance and Reliability."
33. Clarke and Primo, *A Model Discipline*, 13. The term "truth-apt" is quoted from Gabriele Contessa. Contessa summarizes his views on model ontology in Contessa, "Scientific Models and Representation," 121. His discussion of the faithfulness and faithlessness of epistemic representation is engaging, if not fully convincing; 127–30. In a discussion of the evident limitations on the authority of scientific models, Nancy Cartwright observes that even with an excellent model, outcomes hold only *ceteris paribus* (all other conditions remaining the same); Cartwright, "Scientific Models versus Social Reality," 335.
34. Apostel, "Towards the Formal Study of Models in the Non-Formal Sciences."
35. Clarke and Primo, *A Model Discipline*, 14; the four model functions are explicated on 83–98.

36. Baden-Fuller and Morgan, "Business Models as Models."
37. And encyclopedias: *Encyclopedia of Business*; Frigg and Hartmann, "Models in Science."
38. Stevenson, *Operations Management*, 19.
39. Dictionary.com, http://www.dictionary.com/browse/ethics?s=t.
40. Frankfurt, *On Bullshit*, 53–56.
41. Classic discussions of models as metaphors and caricatures include Black, *Models and Metaphors*; Gibbard and Varian, "Economic Models." The model as fiction is more prominent in later discussions, as for example in Giere, "How Models Are Used to Represent Reality"; Frigg, "Models and Fiction"; Mäki, "Models and the Locus of Their Truth"; Levy. "Fictional Models *de novo* and *de re*"; Portides, "How Scientific Models Differ from Works of Fiction."
42. Morgan and Morrison, "Introduction," in *Models as Mediators*, 11–12.
43. Echenique, "Models," 27.
44. Schmidt, "The Physics of Climate Modeling."
45. On the agency of dolls' houses as models, see Wharton, "Doll's House/Dollhouse."
46. Huizinga, *Homo Ludens*.
47. Some of Huizinga's stipulations for play are less applicable: its amorality and impracticality. Those who cite Huizinga's classic text without recognizing its politics have missed its point. Huizinga, *Homo Ludens*, 206.
48. Huizinga, *Homo Ludens*, 10.

2. Body Model/Science/History

I am grateful to Valeria Finucci for her comments on this chapter. I am indebted as well to the great multiplate etcher Johnny Friedländer, who taught me the printing skills which are herein discussed.

1. The human body still offers considerable resistance to monetization, though it sometimes succumbs to it. Wilson, "UCLA Suspends Its Willed Body Program," CNN, March 9, 2004, http://www.cnn.com/2004/LAW/03/09/ucla.cadaver.suit/index.html. More broadly, see Chaney, *Body Brokers*.
2. Obesity is not the only grounds for rejection. The Mayo Clinic's list is typical: emaciation, contamination with an infectious disease, mutilation (autopsy or sustained injuries), and delivery of the body after forty-eight hours. Mayo Clinic, "Body Donation at Mayo Clinic." Though not listed

on the Mayo Clinic website, bodies that are too tall are also unacceptable in most programs; they don't fit on standard gurneys.
3. Rich, "This Is the Place Where Death Delights to Help the Living."
4. For example, Choulant, *History and Bibliography of Anatomic Illustration*; Roberts and Tomlinson, *The Fabric of the Body*; Kemp and Wallace, *Spectacular Bodies*; Meli, *Visualizing Disease*.
5. On anatomical models' incorporation of cultural assumptions, see Fleck, *Genesis and Development of a Scientific Fact*.
6. Black, *A Descriptive, Analytical, and Critical Catalogue*. The Bodleian also offers an excellent digital facsimile, available online at https://digital.bodleian.ox.ac.uk/inquire/p/b3c5b023-c431-4a4b-adcf-c407a1a7886d. Generally, for the mutual dependence of scientific development and image technology, Daston and Galison, *Objectivity*.
7. "Hic stat semen creatus; hic nutrit infans & crescit; hic cadat semen & cum ceciderit colliguntur testiculi in se." I am grateful for James Rives's suggested corrections to my translation. For a clear transcription of all the labels, see Singer, "A Thirteenth-Century Drawing of the Anatomy of the Uterus and Adnexa."
8. *Acland's Video Atlas of Human Anatomy* is discussed later in the chapter.
9. For an example, Billings, *Architectural Illustrations of Kettering Church*, pl. 6.
10. The recension is known as the Fünfbilderserie, established by Karl Sudhoff early in the twentieth century. Sudhoff, "Anatomische Zeichnungen aus dem 12. und 13. Jahrhundert" *and* "Abermals eine neue Handschrift der anatomischen Fünfbilderserie"; O'Neill, "The Fünfbilderserie"; Taylor McCall, "Reliquam dicit pictura." The set of illuminations with which Ashmole 399 has the most in common is Gonville and Caius College, Cambridge, Ms 190/223. That manuscript dates from the twelfth century.
11. For the most explicit articulation of his method, see Weitzmann, *Illustrations in Roll and Codex*. For a critical description of Weitzmann's method, see Vikan, "Ruminations on Edible Icons," 48.
12. For an amusing summary of philology's history, see Lernout, "The Angel of Philology." He writes about philologists, "In Dutch we used to call them 'kommaneukers,' *comma fuckers*," 48
13. For the precarity of relationships between medical images and medical texts, see Jones, "Image, Word and Medicine in the Middle Ages."
14. Ferckel, "Weitere Beiträge zur Geschichte der Anatomie im Mittelalter"; Handerson, *Gilbertus Anglicus*.

15. Ambrosetti, "Algorithmic in the 12th Century."
16. For dating, see MacKinney and Bober, "A Thirteenth-Century Medical Case History in Miniatures."
17. The mummified torso turned up in a medical antiquities market in 2003. Charlier et al., "A Glimpse into the Early Origins of Medieval Anatomy."
18. Celsus, *On Medicine* [*De medicina*], 1:23–27
19. In the year 765. Bliquez and Kazhdan, "Four Testimonia to Human Dissection in Byzantine Times," 555.
20. Park, *Secrets of Women*, 39–42. For an account of the canonization proceedings, see Menestò, "Il Processo apostolico per la canonizzazione di Chiara da Montefalco." Also, Dejure, "La 'Legenda' volgare di santa Chiara da Montefalco." For a compelling treatment of medieval body parts, see Bynum, *Fragmentation and Redemption*.
21. For an excellent introduction to the subject, see Park, "The Criminal and the Saintly Body." Also see Green, "From 'Diseases of Women' to 'Secrets of Women.'"
22. During a class discussion of 13v of Ashmole 399 at Duke University, an undergraduate computer science major asked, "When did people learn to draw?"
23. Demystified by Park, *Secrets of Women*, 272–73, n. 20.
24. Matthias Schemmel, in his discussion of the effects of medieval diagrams on later scientific thinking, suggests that in the "process of knowledge transformation, the medieval diagrams . . . served as catalysts of conceptual development." Schemmel, "Medieval Representations of Change and Their Early Modern Application," 32.
25. Vesalius, *De humani corporis fabrica*.
26. Those who have written about these images often give Vesalius credit for them by not identifying the artist. Symptomatic is Harcourt, "Andreas Vesalius and the Anatomy of Antique Sculpture." Except in a final, dismissive footnote, Harcourt referred to the artist throughout his piece as "the draftsman," which, like "draft horse," implies a certain slavishness. For antidotes, see Panofsky, "Artist, Scientist, Genius." William Ivins identifies Vesalius as a fraud, whose fame depended on the theft of John Stephen of Calcars's plates. Ivins, "*A Propos* of the 'Fabrica' of Vesalius." For a balanced art-historical assessment, see Kemp, "A Drawing for the 'Fabrica.'" Kemp concludes: "At present, we cannot categorically assert that the ability to achieve such a standard lay either within or outside the scope of the

little-known Kalkar; but the documentary and visual evidence is gently inclined in favor of his authorship of the muscle-men," 288.
27. Still one of the most insightful treatments of the effect of printing on cultural production is Latour, "Visualization and Cognition." Also see Eisenstein, *The Printing Revolution in Early Modern Europe*, and McKitterick, *Print, Manuscript and the Search for Order*.
28. Kusukawa, *Picturing the Book of Nature*.
29. Vesalius's frontispiece is the first illustration in two of the most recent anglophone works on the subject of art and anatomization. Finucci, "Vesalius and the Languages of Anatomy"; Graciano, *Visualizing the Body in Art, Anatomy, and Medicine*.
30. Vesalius, *De humani corporis fabrica*, 5.15, 539.
31. Park, "The Criminal and the Saintly Body," 12.
32. Heseler, *Andreas Vesalius' First Public Anatomy at Bologna*, 71, nn. 34 and 35.
33. Ferrari, "Public Anatomy Lessons and the Carnival."
34. For an overview of grave robbing, see Sappol, *A Traffic of Dead Bodies*.
35. Vesalius, *De humani corporis fabrica*, 5.15, 538–39.
36. Ivins, "What about the 'Fabrica' of Vesalius?'"; Lambert, "The Initial Letters of the Anatomical Treatise."
37. Other illicit practices are depicted in these initials. For example, in the letter "O" bones are boiled in a caldron. To what degree the boiling of bones went against the decrees of the Catholic Church is subject to a debate focused on Pope Boniface VIII's bull "De Sepulturis," issued in 1300, which forbade the boiling of bones. The bull's title sentence may be translated: "Persons cutting up the bodies of the dead, barbarously cooking them in order that the bones being separated from the flesh may be carried for burial into their own countries are by the very fact excommunicated." Merrigan, "Anatomy," 459.
38. For a revolting account of the abuse of the dead during dissection, see MacDonald, *Human Remains*.
39. Paley, *Natural Theology*, 202.
40. Peirce, "Lessons of the History of Science."
41. Still one of the clearest and cleverest discussions of the distinction between analog and digital: Haugeland, "Analog and Analog."
42. The gravid (from the Latin *gravidus*, heavy) uterus is the pregnant uterus. Hunter, *Anatomia uteri humani gravidi tabulis illustrata*; Thornton and

NOTES TO PAGES 38–42

Want, "Jan van Rymsdyk's Illustrations of the Gravid Uterus"; Gamer, "Scalpel to Burin."
43. The vertical measure of the etched womb is 11 inches; horizontal is 8.5 inches.
44. It is tempting to discuss this image in terms of Edmund Burke's sublime.
45. See, among many works, Kemp, *Leonardo*. For an unfair dismissal of all other anatomical artists, Ackerman, "Leonardo da Vinci."
46. Brock, *Dr. William Hunter's Papers and Drawings*.
47. Jordanova, "Gender, Generation, and Science."
48. For a clear summary of printing history with bibliography, see Sappol, *Dream Anatomy*. The copperplate etching was in its turn replaced as the most popular means of reproducing reality first by the lithograph and then by the photograph and offset printing. Frank Netter's extraordinarily popular (still now) anatomical renderings offer perfect examples of the latter. Netter, *The Ciba Collection of Medical Illustrations*.
49. Hunter was a licentiate of the Royal College of Physicians in London, but never elected a member. He unsuccessfully tried to force the issue both through an organized attack on one of the membership meetings and, subsequently, through litigation. Simmons and Hunter, *William Hunter*, xi.
50. Bell, "Theater of Anatomy, Great Windmill Street," 99.
51. Hunter, *Dr. William Hunter at the Royal Academy of Arts*, 39.
52. Kemp, "True to Their Natures."
53. Glasgow University Library, Special Collections, q 860z 1783–5, mounted between pp. 16 and 17. Quoted from Martin Kemp's introduction to Hunter, *Dr. William Hunter at the Royal Academy of Arts*, 16.
54. Hunter, *Dr. William Hunter at the Royal Academy of Arts*, 15–17.
55. Farre, "Advertisement for Morbid Anatomy."
56. For an excellent account of dissection, preservation, and display practices in eighteenth-century England, see Mitchell, *Anatomical Dissection in Enlightenment England and Beyond*.
57. Morgan, "The Art of Making Anatomical Preparations by Corrosion," 371.
58. This extraordinary memoire with entries from 1763 to 1809 is wonderfully revealing of the life of a medical practitioner in the eighteenth century, as well as of English attitudes toward the unrest and then revolution in the American colonies. Knyveton, *Man Midwife*, 68.
59. Sheppard, *The Parish of St. James Westminster*, 48–50; plan, pl. 135c in pt. 2, vol. 32. For Hunter's diagram of his space, see Hunter, *Two Introductory Lectures Delivered by Dr. William Hunter*, after p. 122.

60. Hunter, *Two Introductory Lectures*, 110.
61. "I should with no student engage in dissections, till he had first attended a complete course of demonstrations.... But, when once he is prepared for this part of his education, he cannot dissect too much." Hunter, *Two Introductory Lectures*, 108.
62. Hunter, *Two Introductory Lectures*, 111.
63. Gannal, *History of Embalming and of Preparation*, 143.
64. For the museum: McCulloch, Russell, and McDonald, *William Hunter's Gravid Uterus*; McCormack, "Housing the Collection"; Chaplin, "Anatomy and the 'Museum Oeconomy.'"
65. Fabricius, *Briefe aus London vermischten Inhalts*, 85–87. I am grateful to Gigi Dillon for her correction of my translation.
66. Date of the will, July 23, 1781; date that the will was proved, April 4, 1783. It included his "house in Windmill Street aforesaid, my Museum, Theater and all offices and buildings whatsoever thereto belong or near adjoining with them and every of their rights...." Hunter, "Will of William Hunter."
67. MacKie, "William Hunter and Captain Cook."
68. Fabricius, *Briefe aus London*, 90.
69. Impey and MacGregor, *The Origins of Museums*. If I called them male versions of a woman's doll's house, this is not a disparagement of cabinets of curiosities, but a reestimation of the doll's house. Wharton, "Doll's House/Dollhouse."
70. For a perfect introduction to Hunter as a collector, see Campbell and Flis, *William Hunter and the Anatomy of the Modern Museum*.
71. Many of the original Hunterian Museum's specimens are now on display in Glasgow. There they work primarily as historical lessons rather than clinical ones.
72. Certainly the publication in which the plate later appeared was a work of remarkable bibliophilic luxury. In the currency of 2018, its original cost was well over $1,000. The volume was not a functional set of images for use by practitioners, but rather a special edition for connoisseurs and collectors. For the price: "The Anatomy of the Human Gravid Uterus," *Derby Mercury*, December 9 (1774), 4.
73. Wharton, *Architectural Agents*, chaps. 1 and 2.
74. Martin and von Daacke. "President's Commission on Slavery and the University." This report also provides a bibliography on the shocking continued exploitation of African Americans after death. Also see Halperin, "The Poor, the Black, and the Marginalized."

75. Knyveton, *Man Midwife*, 35–36.
76. "Another Graveyard Plundered," *Boston Commercial Gazette*, January 19, 1824; "Riot," *Carolina Sentinel*, February 21, 1824.
77. McCracken-Flesher, *The Doctor Dissected*; Rosner, *The Anatomy Murders*.
78. Arnold, *The Spaces of the Hospital*.
79. "The Numbers of Objects under Cure the Last Year in the Several Hospitals and Infirmaries of This Metropolis," *The Gentleman's Magazine* 18, May 1748, 198.
80. Most hyperbolically by Shelton, "The Emperor's New Clothes." For dismissal of Shelton's claims, see, among many others, King, "History without Historians?"
81. Hunter, *Two Introductory Lectures*, 117–20.
82. McDonald and Faithfull, "William Hunter's Sources of Pathological and Anatomical Specimens."
83. Hunter, *Two Introductory Lectures*, 113.
84. Hunter, *Two Introductory Lectures*, 113.
85. For the United States, Blake, "The Development of American Anatomy Acts"; Hall, "The Catholic Brahmin and the Anatomy Act of 1898."
86. In England, bodies were "objects." In the United States into the twentieth century they were often referred to as "material." Jenkins, "The Legal Status of Dissecting."
87. Sappol, *Traffic*; Richardson, "Bentham and 'Bodies for Dissection.'"
88. Knyveton, *Man Midwife*, 66.
89. Gannal, *History of Embalming and of Preparation*, 200 and n. 13. A summary of historical embalming practices precedes a description of the author's own experiments in embalming. More recent discussions of embalming are more narrowly technological, e.g., Hayashi et al., "History and Future of Cadaver Preservation for Surgical Training."
90. Brenner, "Human Body Preservation."
91. Henry et al., "Consensus Guidelines for the Uniform Reporting of Study Ethics."
92. "First Day in Gross Anatomy Lab," https://web.duke.edu/anatomy/siteParts/dukeVideos/FirstDayInTheGrossAnatomyLab-2013.mp4. For a full description of an anatomy class, see Montross, *Body of Work*.
93. Jones, "Bioethical Aspects of Commemorations and Memorials."
94. Marmoy, "The 'Auto-Icon' of Jeremy Bentham."
95. I met him again at the Met Breuer in New York in 2018. Syson et al., "Life Like."

96. Cornwall et al., "Who Donates Their Body to Science?"; Garment et al., "Let the Dead Teach the Living." Body parts continue to circulate in the market. Champney, "The Business of Bodies."
97. This dependence of body donation on the acceptance of cremation seems to have gone largely unnoted. Reference to the cremation of remains is avoided in the description of the body donation program of the Sackler Faculty of Medicine, Tel Aviv University. "Burial." Where cremation is still abhorred, body donation is limited.
98. In anatomical literature from premodernity to the present, religion is largely absent. There are, of course, exceptions. Bell, *The Hand*.
99. There was always strong opposition. For Bentham's role in getting the act passed, see Richardson, "Bentham and 'Bodies for Dissection.'"
100. Brummitt, "*Protestant Relics*."
101. Schmitz-Esser, *Der Leichnam im Mittelalter*.
102. Prothero, *Purified by Fire*, 15. It is important to note that the popularization of cremation coincided with the removal of the dead from within cities to their peripheries. Strauss, *Human Remains*, 2–3.
103. Parliament (United Kingdom), "Cremation Act 1902." For the legalization of cremation in the United States, see Prothero, *Purified by Fire*.
104. Its owner rebuilt it immediately in an undisclosed location. Wagner, "Israel's Only Crematorium to Re-Open," *Jerusalem Post*, October 28, 2007.
105. I am not, of course, referring here to the anatomy lab's representations in popular books or in the media—from serious depictions, like that of Paul Kalanithi, to absurd renderings, like that in the soap opera *Grey's Anatomy*. Kalanithi, *When Breath Becomes Air*; Ellen Pompeo, dir., "Season 14, Episode 15: Old Scars, Future Hearts," of *Grey's Anatomy* (March 15, 2018).
106. McIsaac, "Gunther von Hagens' Body Worlds"; Waldby, *The Visible Human Project*; Newman, "Susan Potter Will Live Forever."
107. Acland, *Acland's Video Atlas of Human Anatomy*.
108. It could be argued that eighteenth-century waxworks are more effective models of the human interior than many contemporary computational ones. "Venerina" (Little Venus) by Clement Susini was such a careful replica of the human body from which it was modeled that physicians used it in 2010 to diagnose the probable cause of her original referent's death. Mazzotti et al., "The Diagnosis of the Cause of the Death of Venerina."
109. The best-known contemporary text on the simulacrum is Baudrillard, "The Precession of Simulacra." Camille, "Simulacrum," offers an elegant

assessment of the history of attitudes toward the representation of that which is not there. The simulacrum's status has shifted from its denunciation in antiquity and the Middle Ages, to its erasure in the early modern, and finally to its embrace in the postmodern and Anthropocene.

110. Certainly, human cadavers elicit a different reaction than holograms from those who study them: "They'll say goodbye to the lab and their cadaver.... They'll hold a memorial service, where they might sing songs or read poems. And then they'll move on to the next course, and the next one. But as they learn about the kidneys or the lungs or the heart, it's his they'll picture." Der Bedrosian, "First-Year Medical Students Still Rely on Cadavers," 9.

111. Zamierowski, Carver, and Guerra, US Patent 9892659B2; Chung et al., "Peeled and Piled Volume Models of the Stomach"; Shen et al., "High-Fidelity Medical Training Model"; Smith et al., "The Role of Anatomy Demonstrators."

112. But extremely powerful as diagnostic devices. Farahani et al., "Three Dimensional Imaging and Scanning."

113. A clever and amusing popular book provides an excellent introduction to cadavers and their current uses: Roach, *Stiff*.

114. As Shogo Hayashi of the Department of Anatomy, Tokyo Medical University, writes, "Fresh-frozen cadaver is currently the model [for surgical training] that is closest to reality." Surgeons, who were traditionally trained on the job with anesthetized live bodies, now, because of increasing patient scrutiny of what is done to them and by whom, need to develop their skills on cadavers. Hayashi et al., "History and Future of Cadaver Preservation for Surgical Training," 449.

115. MacDonald, *Human Remains*. Public dissections of human bodies are no longer licit. Those of P. T. Barnum and Gunther van Hagen have been officially entitled "autopsies" for legal purposes.

3. Building Model/Architecture/Politics

1. Of course, occasionally a model's politics are too explicit to be ignored, as in the case cited in the epigraph. Weizman, *Hollow Land*, 195–96.
2. Peter Eisenman, "Poetics of the Model: Eisenman's Doubt. An Interview with Peter Eisenman by David Shapiro and Lindsay Stamm on March 8, 1981," in Eisenman, Pommer, and Hubert, *Idea as Model*, 121–25.
3. For the political and the abject, Feinstein, "Zbigniew Libera's Lego Concentration Camp."

4. Treating the empty tomb of Jesus in chapter 3 is also, in a peculiar way, complementary to the discussion of the cadaver in chapter 2.
5. For the divisions of the space and their history, see Cust, *The Status Quo in the Holy Places*.
6. For accessible descriptions of the building's complexity, see Ousterhout, "Architecture as Relic and the Construction of Sanctity"; Ousterhout, "Is Nothing Sacred?"
7. For a fuller discussion this church, including the historiographic debate about the Temple Church's referent, see Wharton, *Selling Jerusalem*, chap. 2.
8. For a short, smart introduction to models in antiquity, see Haselberger, "Architectural Likenesses." I am grateful to Emily Mohr for this reference.
9. Klinkenberg, *Compressed Meanings*; Brubaker, "Gifts and Prayers."
10. Lewer and Dark, *The Temple Church in London*.
11. Godfrey, "Recent Discoveries at the Temple, London." The earlier version of the nave was similar to that of the Templars' church of their Paris commandery, as it has been reconstructed. Curzon, *La maison du temple de Paris*, 7.
12. Folda, *The Art of the Crusaders in the Holy Land*, 175–245. Also see Vincent and Abel, *Jérusalem*, vol. 2, fasc. 1–3.
13. Dove, "The Temple Church and Its Restoration."
14. The Templar rule stipulates that the Order should follow the liturgy of the Holy Sepulchre. However, it has been suggested on the basis of manuscripts from Modena and Cambridgeshire, that Templar churches in Europe adopted the local liturgy. Dondi, *The Liturgy of the Canons Regular of the Holy Sepulchre of Jerusalem*, 41–42; Linder, "The Liturgy of the Liberation of Jerusalem."
15. Chaplain of Sir Richard Guylforde, *Pylgrymage of Sir Richard Guylforde to the Holy Land*, 24.
16. Like its counterpart in Paris, the London Temple was intimately tied to the monarchy, serving on occasion as the king's treasury or safety deposit. Delisle, *Mémoire sur les opérations financières des Templiers*.
17. Brown, *The Da Vinci Code*.
18. The Hospitallers, though founded earlier than the Templars, were only militarized later. See Riley-Smith, *Hospitallers*.
19. Butler and Dafoe, *The Warriors and the Bankers*. The frankly absurd thesis of the book is that the Templars, being good bankers, fled France with their wealth before the Order's destruction in 1307. Establishing

NOTES TO PAGES 62–67

themselves in Switzerland, they became the progenitors of Protestantism and capitalism.

20. Prawer, *The Latin Kingdom of Jerusalem*; Metcalf, "The Templars as Bankers."
21. Bernard of Clairvaux, *La Règle du Temple*, 45; *The Rule of the Templars*, 29.
22. Once located over the south entrance, the Latin dedicatory inscription was destroyed during restorations in 1695 after being repeatedly defaced by righteous Protestants. A copy of its transcription now appears on the west wall of the church in the entrance arch. The translation here is a slightly modified version of that which appears in Williamson, *The History of the Temple, London*, 11, n. 2.
23. In the Middle Ages, it was sometimes referred to as the New Temple because it replaced the earlier, smaller Templar church in its first London enclosure at Holborn. That church was not demolished until 1595. Lewer and Dark, *The Temple Church in London*.
24. Krautheimer, "Introduction to an 'Iconography of Medieval Architecture.'"
25. Krautheimer, "Introduction to an 'Iconography of Medieval Architecture,'" 17.
26. Externally about 4.3 m long, 2.4 m wide, and 3 m high.
27. YHESVM OVERITIS NAZARENVM CRUCIFIXUM SVRREXIT NON EST HIC ECCE LOCVS VBI POSVERVNT EVM. Sperling, "Leon Battista Alberti's Inscriptions on the Holy Sepulchre."
28. IOHANNES RVCELLARIVS/PAVLI·F·VTINDE SALVTEM SVAM/PRECARETVRVNDE OMNIVM CVM/CHRISTO FACTA EST RESVRECTIO/SACELLVM HOC/ADISTAR IHEROSOLIMITANI SEPVL/CHRI FACIVNDVM CVRAVIT/MCCCCLXVII. I want to thank James B. Rives for his translation of this inscription. For alternative translations, see Braun, "The Politics of Immortality" and Robert Tavernor, *On Alberti and the Art of Building*, 115.
29. Vasari, *Le vite de' più eccellenti architetti, pittori, et scultori Italiani*, 1.2.366–70; Vasari, "Leon Batista Alberti," 3:44–45.
30. Burckhardt, *The Civilization of the Renaissance in Italy*, 136–38.
31. "Leon Battista Alberti." Wikipedia, 2016, https://en.wikipedia.org/wiki/Leon_Battista_Alberti.
32. Alberti continues to be celebrated in scholarly literature dealing with buildings and proportional systems. For example, in *Architecture and Mathematics from Antiquity to the Future*, Kim Williams is the only name that appears on more pages than that of Alberti. Williams and Ostwald, *Architecture and Mathematics from Antiquity to the Future*.

33. Bardeschi, "Nuove ricerche sul S. Sepolcro nella Cappella Rucellai a Firenze"; Naujokat, "Ut rhetorica architectura"; Pintore, "Musical Symbolism in the Works of Leon Battista Alberti"; Sperling, "Leon Battista Alberti's Inscriptions." The most elaborate measurements are recorded in the illustrations in Bonora, Tucci, and Vaccaro, "3D Data Fusion and Multi-Resolution Approach for a New Survey."
34. Alberti, *De re aedificatoria*. Quotations come from the English edition, Alberti, *On the Art of Building in Ten Books*.
35. Alberti, *On the Art of Building in Ten Books*, 200 (bk. 7.5).
36. Alberti, *On the Art of Building in Ten Books*, 303 (bk. 9.5).
37. According to his will, the site of the tomb within the chapel was to be determined by his sons. Pacciani, "Alberti a Firenze," 240. Also see Kent, "The Making of a Renaissance Patron of the Arts," 94.
38. Heydenreich, "Die Cappella Rucellai von San Pancrazio in Florence," 222–25. For a subtle critique of Heydenreich's proposition, see Krautheimer, "Commentary on Heydenreich's Observations in 'Die Cappella Rucellai und die Badia Fiesolana.'"
39. Tavernor, *On Alberti and the Art of Building*, 110. Also see Nagel and Wood, *Anachronic Renaissance*, 168.
40. Rucellai, *Giovanni Rucellai ed il suo "Zibaldone,"* 1:135. Tavernor does acknowledge "that there is some doubt about the authenticity of this letter." Tavernor, *On Alberti and the Art of Building*, 110. Others have cited the letter to make their arguments stronger; e.g., de Klerck, "Jerusalem in Renaissance Italy," 229. Nagel and Wood would love to accept the forger's fiction. "Even if true [that the document is a forgery], the letters may yet transmit elements of lost originals." Nagel and Wood, *Anachronic Renaissance*, 410, n. 20.
41. Kent, "The Letters Genuine and Spurious of Giovanni Rucellai."
42. An exception is Mele, "Il Sacello del Santo Sepolcro nella Cappella Rucellai."
43. Wilkinson, *Jerusalem Pilgrimage 1099–1185*, 170–71.
44. Kempe, *The Book of Margery Kempe*, 73.
45. Wey, Williams, and Bulkeley, *The Itineraries of William Wey*, xxviii–xxx.
46. Shalev, "Christian Pilgrimage and Ritual Measurement in Jerusalem."
47. For the index's physical contiguity with its referent, see Atkin, "Peirce on the Index and Indexical Reference."
48. Pope Paul II's bull was included in Giovanni Rucellai's *Zibaldone*. The text is reproduced in Perosa, *Giovanni Rucellai ed il suo "Zibaldone,"* 1:24–25.

49. British Museum OA10339, 45 cm/17.7 in × 38 cm/14.9 in × 26.5 cm/10.4 in.
50. I had no difficulty taking the model apart, but needed curatorial help in putting it back together. For a demonstration, see McMahon, "British Museum Takes Apart 1600s Model of the Holy Sepulchre."
51. Several models of the Church of the Nativity in Bethlehem also exist, as well as many independent models of the aedicule. For the beautifully illustrated corpus of all these objects, see Piccirillo, *La Nuova Gerusalemme*. How hard it is for a model to survive is suggested by the loss of two of the three models described in a 1920 article: Dalman, "Die Modelle der Grabeskirche und Grabeskapelle in Jerusalem." Another model of the Holy Sepulchre, contributed to the collection by Queen Victoria, has disappeared from the Victoria and Albert Museum. Leslie, "Inside Outside," 168–69. For the British Museum series, Williams et al., "Sacred Souvenir."
52. Dalman's section of the model in Augsburg (now lost) may be compared with the section by Bernardino Amico in his *Trattato*, pl. 24. Dalman, "Die Modelle der Grabeskirche und Grabeskapelle in Jerusalem," fig. 2.
53. Alberti, *On the Art of Building in Ten Books*, 34 (bk. 2.1), 154–55 (bk. 6.1), 296–97 (bk. 9.3), 317 (bk. 9.10)
54. Alberti, *On the Art of Building in Ten Books*, 38 (bk. 2.4).
55. Alberti, *On the Art of Building in Ten Books*, 318 (bk. 9.11).
56. Alberti, *On the Art of Building in Ten Books*. The term *adstitores* is translated as "clerks of works," by Rykwert et al., Alberti's translators, but the only contemporary or earlier instances of the word that I have found are in the context of ecclesiastical officialdom.
57. For a concise and critical description of the change in architectural practice from medieval to Early Modern, see Trachtenberg, "To Build Proportions in Time, or Tie Knots in Space?" For a fuller statement of this argument, see his *Building-in-Time*.
58. Carpo, *The Alphabet and the Algorithm*, 26. Carpo, among others, designates Alberti as a cardinal figure in the cultural revolution that shaped architectural modernity, characterized as the alienation of the design of a building from its construction.
59. Suppes and Scott, "Foundational Aspects of Theories of Measurement," 113.
60. See the discussion of printing in the previous chapter. In addition, Carpo, *Architecture in the Age of Printing*.
61. The model's history before the bequest is unknown. Allison Siegenthaler, curatorial administrator of Britain, Europe, and Prehistory (BEP) and

Africa, Oceania, and the Americas (AOA) collections at the British Museum, London, email, July 1, 2019.

62. For Amico's chronology, see Bagatti, "Introduction." Perspective drawings of the exteriors of Palestine's sacred places were first widely distributed through the publication in German and Latin of Bernhard von Breydenbach, *Peregrinatio in terram sanctam*. Handsome analytic drawings were also presented in *Il devotissimo viaggio di Gerusalemme* in 1587 by Zuallart (who signed his work as Giovanni Zuallardo Cavalliere del Santissimo Sepolchro [Knight of the Most Holy Sepulchre]). For a discussion of Zuallart's renderings, see Russo, "The Printed Illustration of Medieval Architecture in Pre-Enlightenment Europe." It should be noted that figs. 13–14 in Russo represent the Church of the Nativity, not as labeled, the Tomb of the Virgin.
63. Amico, *Trattato*, 1st and 2nd eds.
64. Amico, *Plans of the Sacred Edifices of the Holy Land*, 96–98.
65. Amico, *Trattato*, 2nd ed., fig. 43.
66. Amico, *Plans of the Sacred Edifices of the Holy Land*, 110.
67. See note 52, above, on Dalman's section.
68. Piccirillo, "The Role of the Franciscans in the Translation of the Sacred Spaces"; Bagatti, "L'industria della madreperla a Betlemme."
69. Jotischky, "The Franciscan Return to the Holy Land."
70. Alston, "Way of the Cross"; Thurston, *The Stations of the Cross*.
71. The scorn rubbed off on Catholics, as famously represented by Erasmus. Erasmus, "Colloquies."
72. Wharton, "Relics, Protestants, Things."
73. That the demise of early modern pilgrimage has been exaggerated is convincingly argued by Noonan, *The Road to Jerusalem*.
74. Think of the "Lamp of Sacrifice," the first chapter in Ruskin, *The Seven Lamps of Architecture*.
75. Viallet, "The Name of God, the Name of Saints, the Name of the Order." The British Museum example prominently exhibits the Name of Jesus and the Jerusalem Cross. The Name of Jesus emblem was popularized by Bernardino da Siena, an acclaimed Franciscan preacher and proto-Savonarola. His use of a panel painted with the symbol of Jesus's name in a sunburst in his performances led to accusations idolatry. He was found guiltless and later canonized. Michelson, "Bernardino of Siena Visualizes the Name of God." Another Franciscan, Saint Bonaventure, author of the canonical version of the life of Saint Francis (alternatives were burned),

adopted the Name of Jesus as his insignia. The Name of Jesus was also later appropriated by the Jesuits, though as Carol Mason warns "IHS should not automatically be construed as a sign of Jesuit involvement." Mason, "Reading the Rings," 8.

76. Gieben, *Lo stemma francescano*.
77. Magni, *Quanto di più curioso e vago ha potuto vedere Cornelio Magna*, 275–76. The rough translation is my own. A less cheerful account of the workers and their Franciscan patrons is given by Frederik Hasselquist, a Lutheran naturalist collecting specimens in the Levant between 1749 and 1752, who comments explicitly on the production and distribution of the models. "[Bethlehem craftsmen] force [the Franciscans] to buy a quantity of Paternosters [beads], models of the grave of Christ, crosses and other wares of this kind, which is the only employ of all the inhabitants of this village. Of these [the Franciscans] have so large a stock in Jerusalem, that the Procurator told me, he had to the value of 15,000 piasters of relics [in the German edition: *Heiligthümer*] in the magazine [storehouse] of the Convent; a sum which one would scarcely believe could be expended on such things. An incredible quantity of them goes yearly to all the Roman Catholic countries in Europe, but most to Spain and Portugal. . . . A number is yearly sent to the Monks [i.e., the Franciscans] in Jerusalem, to be given as presents to the patrons of their order; and these are best paid for by other presents they receive in return." Hasselquist, *Voyages and Travels in the Levant*, 148–49. Bellarmino Bagatti cites further Early Modern travelers' accounts of the artisans' work and their ties to the Franciscan monastery in Bethlehem. Bagatti, "L'industria della madreperla a Betlemme."
78. Piccirillo, "Miniatura do Santo Sepulchro de Jerusalém."
79. Piccirillo, *La Nuova Gerusalemme*, 57–58.
80. Amico, *Trattato*, 2nd ed., pls. 21 and 45.
81. Bagatti, "Introduction," 4–8. Since the British mapping of Jerusalem's topography in the late nineteenth century, most archaeologists recognize the legitimacy of the Franciscans' argument. See Warren, *The Temple or the Tomb*.
82. Amico, *Plans of the Sacred Edifices of the Holy Land*, 38–39.
83. Colin Powell used the slide in his report to the United Nations Security Council on February 5, 2003, as part of the lead-up to the invasion of Iraq. See https://georgewbush-whitehouse.archives.gov/news/releases/2003/02/powell-slides/31.html.
84. Issued November 19, 1544. Setton, *The Papacy and the Levant*, 3:142–97, 486. Also see O'Banion, "Only the King Can Do It."

85. Lemmens, *Acta S. Congregationis de Propaganda Fide pro Terra Sancta*, 231; Piccirillo, "Un modellino della Basilica del Santo Sepolcro de Gerusalemme conservato a Malta," 73. The rough translation is my own. The passage ends with a note that the Grand Vizier Köprülüzade Fazil Ahmed Pasha had died.
86. For a relevant critique of the traditional division between major and minor arts, see Binski, "London, Paris, Assisi, Rome around 1300."
87. After the title of a temporary exhibition of the work by the same name. Williams et al., "Sacred Souvenir."
88. Finch & Co., "'The Pearson' Model of the Church of the Holy Sepulchre, Jerusalem (1600 to 1700)." Antiques and Works of Art. London: Finch & Co, 2020 (2016), https://www.finch-and-co.co.uk/artwork-detail/813262/18678/the-pearson-model-of-the-church-of.
89. For the slow death of the Palestine Archaeological Museum, aka the Rockefeller Museum, see Wharton, *Architectural Agents*, 31–56.
90. Like the splendid example in the Kunsthistorisches Museum in Vienna. After a long and evasive correspondence with the curator in control of the piece in April and May 2015, concerning the model and the possibility of studying it, I received a final reply: "I had now the possibility to talk with our conservators who were in charge to prepare the models transport and its storing in our outside storage. Unfortunately, I have to tell you that the model had to be dismantled for the transport and that every single piece is now packed separately. . . . I'm therefore afraid that we can support you with a photo-documentation of the piece only." Museums are often cruel to the objects they ensnare, but they rarely bury them alive.
91. De Certeau, *The Practice of Everyday Life*, 92.
92. For an insightful investigation of the power of miniaturization, particularly as metaphor, see Stewart, *On Longing*, esp. chap. 2.
93. Avi-Yonah, *A Short Guide to the Model of Ancient Jerusalem*; Avi-Yonah, *Pictorial Guide to the Model of Ancient Jerusalem*; Avi-Yonah and Tsafrir, *Pictorial Guide to the Model of Ancient Jerusalem*; Amit, *Model of Jerusalem in the Second Temple Period*; Tsafrir, "Designing the Model of Jerusalem at the Holy Land Hotel," in Hebrew; Padan, *Modelscapes of Nationalism*. I am grateful to Yoram Tsafrir for giving me a personal tour of the model while it was still at the Holy Land Hotel.
94. Hava Avi-Yonah did much of the work on the design of the buildings in the model; making was done by Erwin Schefler and later by Rolf Brutzen, Baruch Engelhardt, and Haim Peretz.

95. Avi-Yonah and Tsafrir, *Pictorial Guide to the Model of Ancient Jerusalem*, 3.
96. For an extended discussion of the meaning of authenticity both generally and in relation to the model, Padan, *Modelscapes of Nationalism*, 88–98.
97. Avi-Yonah, *A Short Guide to the Model of Ancient Jerusalem*, 3, 8–9.
98. The literature on evangelical Zionism is immense. For an introduction, see Hummel, "His Land and the Origins of the Jewish-Evangelical Israel Lobby."
99. Gordon's nonparochial Protestantism is evident from the company he kept. In Jerusalem, for example, he stayed at the American Colony, an establishment of very charitable, very unorthodox evangelicals, loathed by the establishment Protestants in the city. Vester, *Our Jerusalem*, chap. 8. For a remarkable biographical sketch of Gordon, see Strachey, *Eminent Victorians*, 189–267.
100. For Gordon's identification of the new site, see Gordon, *Reflections in Palestine*, esp. vii–viii. Silberman, *Digging for God and Country*, 152–53; Monk, *An Aesthetic Occupation*, 17–44. Gordon was not the first to identify Golgotha with the declivity near Jeremiah's Grotto. Conder, *Tent Work in Palestine*, 2:332–76.
101. For this group's historical perspective, see Izzett, White, and Hardcastle, *The Garden Tomb Jerusalem*.
102. *Welcome to the Garden Tomb*.
103. For example, O'Dell, "RS Tours." For the Orlando theme park, see Wharton, *Selling Jerusalem*, 223–28.
104. That these names are misplaced is the consensus of archaeologists. For a review of the evidence, see Wharton, "Jerusalem's Zions."
105. Bar, "Recreating Jewish Sanctity in Jerusalem."
106. Avi-Yonah, *A Short Guide to the Model of Ancient Jerusalem*. 6.
107. "The Second Temple Jerusalem Model," *Tripadvisor—Jerusalem, Things to Do*, 2019, https://www.tripadvisor.com/ShowUserReviews-g293983-d324091-r393037289-The_Second_Temple_Jerusalem_Model-Jerusalem_Jerusalem_District.html.
108. For a succinct account of the archaeological and literary evidence of the Temple, see Meyers, "Temple, Jerusalem."
109. Padan, *Modelscapes of Nationalism*, 19.
110. Désilets, "Assassin's Creed."
111. De Sacy, "Mémoire sur la dynastie des Assassins."
112. Spence, "Jesper Kyd and Assassin's Creed."
113. For example, Goldstein. "Assassin's Creed Review"; VanOrd, "Assassin's Creed Is a Beautiful and Exciting Experience."
114. Bradshaw, "Assassin's Creed Review"; Collin, "Assassin's Creed Review."

115. There are other popular games that have taken history seriously: *Oregon Trail, Kingdom Come Deliverance, Total War*. Academic attempts have been made to assess historical accuracy of a particular video game. E.g., Shaw, "The Tyranny of Realism." The most concise and compelling treatment that I have so far encountered is on YouTube: Jewitt. "Accuracy vs. Authenticity in Video Games."
116. Pontbriand. "Making Assassin's Creed Unity."
117. Thier, "Ubisoft Is Giving 'Assassin's Creed Unity Away."
118. Venables, "Exclusive Interview."
119. Jagadheeswari, Gayatri Devi, and Jothi Priya, "Evaluating the Effects of Video Games." Judging from my own in-game stress, I was surprised by the relatively low heart-rate increase of those in the study.
120. Kuo, Hiler, and Lutz, "From Super Mario to Skyrim," 102.
121. The evidence for Kuo, Hiler, and Lutz's article is interviews with gamers, so my personal experience offers a legitimate counterargument.
122. Stephenson, *Snow Crash*; Wachowski and Wachowski, *The Matrix*.

4. BLACK BOXES

1. Hesiod, *Works and Days*, ll. 47–101, and *Theogony*, ll. 558–612, both in *Theogony, Works and Days, Testimonia*.
2. Giannopoulou, *Pithoi*, esp. 27–33; Bevan, "Pandora's Pithos."
3. This "error" in translation is noted in relation to Lilius Giraldus (1580) in an anthropologically sophisticated (for its day) article by Harrison, "Pandora's Box," 100. Harrison's "error" is identified as "philological accident" and ascribed to Erasmus by the Panofskys. Panofsky and Panofsky, *Pandora's Box*, 17–18.
4. "The ancients held religiously to their belief that gifts were to be carefully examined, as to who had sent them and with what intention; since it is well known that anything given by those who wish us ill would usually be for our destruction. It was so with the deceiving box [pyxis] sent to Prometheus by Jove through Pandora; and with the garment which Medea gave to the new wife of Jason, and the garment Deianira sent to Hercules." Erasmus, *Adagia*, 263.
5. Von Hilgers, "The History of the Black Box."
6. Roeder and Creighton, "Reports of Sections and Societies," 296.
7. MacKay, "Towards an Information-Flow Model of Human Behaviour," 30. Or, in a more nuanced form, "Psychology, in so far as it is what we

call 'objective,' is 'black box technique.' By observing what goes in and what comes out, we seek to abstract laws relating them. No such observations, by themselves, can tell us about the machinery inside. Yet the divorce is not absolute; when we know, as we do, something about the internal machinery, further inferences about it can be suggested by 'black box' laws—that is, by input-output relations." Hick, "The Impact of Information Theory on Psychology," 398.

8. Eckert and Jones, *Faster, Faster,* 23.
9. Bunge, "A General Black Box Theory," 347.
10. For an example of the (mis)application of "black box" to architecture in general, see Banham, "A Black Box."
11. This is a variation of the World Health Organization's definition of good health: "Health is a state of complete physical, mental and social well-being and not merely the absence of disease or infirmity." World Health Organization, "Preamble to the Constitution."
12. McPartland, "BIM Dimensions."
13. Kim, "A Pilot of Student-Guided Virtual Reality Tours"; William H. Collinge, "Exploring Construction Project Design as Multimodal Social Semiotic Practice."
14. Yang et al., "Review of Built Heritage Modelling."
15. They lurk still at the margins. And there is resistance to the loss of physical models. The following story was recounted to me by one of Peter Eisenman's students. In 2013 "Thom Mayne crashed Eisenman's review, calling the premise of the whole studio flawed, and was summarily booted. Whereas most all of the eighteen some critics assembled by Eisenman wore black . . . , Mayne [at Yale for another review] was in a leopard-print suit, bright scudded sneakers, and a camo hat. Later on, many of Eisenman's critics rounded into him, calling out what they termed his basswood fetish, deriding it as a dated and infantilizing medium, to which Eisenman retorted something like 'I will be buried in a basswood box.'"
16. The joys if not the financial profits of digital mass customization are described by Carpo, *The Second Digital Turn.*
17. There was much more waste and redundancy before BIM. According to John O'Brien, one-time director of documentation control of Richard Meier's Getty Center project, there were twelve thousand pages of plans, 20 percent of which were changed monthly.
18. And downsides. It is increasingly expensive and technically complacent. AHMM et al., "Open Letter to Andrew Anagnost."

NOTES TO PAGES 107–113   143

19. Augé, *Non-Places*.
20. AutoCAD was, as Autodesk's founder acknowledges, developed to meet a desire for a profitable product, not a desire for better building. Walker, *The Autodesk File*, 9–20. For the irate complaints of architectural offices about Revit's current clunkiness, see AHMM et al., "Open Letter to Andrew Anagnost," and Davis, "Architects versus Autodesk." Davis describes the situation: "Architects have long grumbled about Autodesk's neglect of its leading BIM platform, Revit. Those frustrations seemingly came to a head in recent weeks, catalyzed by the publication of a damning open letter to Autodesk CEO Andrew Anagnost last month from 17 architecture and engineering firms, including Grimshaw, Zaha Hadid Architects, and BVN Architectural Services."
21. Carpo, *The Alphabet and the Algorithm*, 26.
22. Latour and Woolgar, *Laboratory Life*, 243.
23. Latour and Woolgar, *Laboratory Life*, 242.
24. Latour, *Science in Action*, esp. 1–17.
25. The limits of statistical probability are amusingly presented by Spiegelhalter, *The Art of Statistics*.
26. Kirkpatrick, Apuzzo, and Gebrekidan, "Europe Said It Was Pandemic-Ready"; Gurdasani and Ziauddeen, "On the Fallibility of Simulation Models in Informing Pandemic Responses"; Hellewell, Funk, and Eggo, "On the Fallibility of Simulation Models."
27. For a magisterial treatment of the emergence and development of computational models for weather prediction, as well as for the then current resistance to anthropogenic climate change, see Edwards, *A Vast Machine*.
28. Church of England, *Liturgies and Occasional Forms of Prayer*, 17.
29. Patton, *War As I Knew It*, 184–86.
30. Martin, "A Christian Hurricane Prayer."
31. Aristotle, *Meteorologica*; Descartes, *Discours de la methode*.
32. Aristotle, *Meteorologica*, bk. 2, pt. 9.
33. Teague and Gallicchio, *The Evolution of Meteorology*, 11–17. This book raises doubts about contemporary standards of academic writing.
34. Hochfelder, *The Telegraph in America*, 59–72.
35. Sydney Chapman, introduction to Richardson, *Weather Prediction by Numerical Process*, v–x.
36. Richardson, *Weather Prediction by Numerical Process*, 219–20.
37. European Centre for Medium-Range Weather Forecasts, "ECMWF Home."
38. "Has Our Climate Changed?"; Stupart, "How a Season Differs from Year to Year."

39. Staby, "A New Epoch in Natural Science," 106.
40. Among the critiques of climate change science are those that claim that there is no consensus about the problem's human activity. Idso, Carter, and Singer, *Why Scientists Disagree about Global Warming*. Note that no sources later than 2010 are cited in this article.
41. Shaftel, Jackson, and Callery, "Scientific Consensus."
42. Romera et al., "Climate Change Projections of Medicanes."
43. Lutz et al., "Selecting Representative Climate Models for Climate Change Impact Studies."
44. Schmidt, "The Physics of Climate Modeling," 72.
45. Jackson, "The Truth Warming Alarmists Don't Want You to Know."
46. Michaels and Wojick, "Climate Modeling Dominates Climate Science," i.
47. Frankfurt, *On Bullshit*.
48. Hulme, "How Climate Models Gain and Exercise Authority."
49. Of course, the vulnerabilities of climate models are not the only basis of climate change deniers' condemnations. They are expert in developing false news then using it to support their fossil-fuel-sponsored agenda. See "What Pause?" An example is the Heartland Institute's publication, Idso, Carter, and Singer, *Why Scientists Disagree about Global Warming*. The Heartland Institute, which receives funding from the Koch brothers, the tobacco industry, and other problematic sources, works against public education and clean energy initiatives. It planned to send its denunciation of scientific evidence of anthropogenic global warming to all science teachers in America. Curt Stager, a noted paleoclimatologist, provides a disturbing description of the institute and the booklet's authors as well as a persuasive denunciation of its contents. Stager, "Sowing Climate Doubt among Schoolteachers."
50. Berner and Lasaga, "Modeling the Geochemical Carbon Cycle."
51. Schneider, "Climate Modeling," 80.
52. The Intergovernmental Panel on Climate Change is perhaps the single most important source of information on the science of climate change. Established by the United Nations Environment Program (UNEP) and the World Meteorological Organization (WMO), it provides an authoritative international assessment of the scientific aspects of climate change, based on the most recent scientific, technical, and socioeconomic information published worldwide. But its summary for policy makers is impenetrable. Science museums everywhere do an excellent job revealing the history of aerospace exploration, but too many are remarkably silent on the dire

consequences of climate change. NASA still does a great job on its website. Shaftel, Jackson, and Callery, "Scientific Consensus."
53. Thoreau, *Walden*.
54. Dehorn, "Los Gatos High School, Assignments for English 11: September 21–25," 2015, https://www.google.com/url?sa=t&rct=j&q=&esrc=s&source=web&cd=11&cad=rja&uact=8&ved=0ahUKEwiXmaHA9YXUAhVKSyYKHU9pBy84ChAWCCEwAA&url=https%3A%2F%2Fd3jc3ahdjad7x7.cloudfront.net%2FxJTASaHFCenfXUTMtU9Oe23oeazoDAWrnJh99OaETAa5Vb8R.docx&usg=AFQjCNG7BPr4-Q7hs-YZhroti_Q_2pHwHA.
55. Skinner, *Walden Two*.
56. Max Black has famously equated models with metaphors. Black, *Models and Metaphors*. Though this generative argument is made for a good cause (i.e., a more productive relationship between the sciences and the humanities), it does not hold up to scrutiny.
57. Cheeseman et al., "Way-Finding in Displaced Clock-Shifted Bees."
58. Viewers of the Stettheimer doll's house in the Museum of the City of New York often don't consult its accompanying wall label because they assume that they already know what they are seeing. This suggests that at least some models might be better off with texts than without them. Wharton, "Doll's House/Dollhouse."
59. Foucault's work is complemented by that of others, including Stewart Hall and Bruno Latour. Foucault, *Discipline and Punish*; Hall, *Representation*; Latour, *Reassembling the Social*.
60. Jebeile and Kennedy, "Explaining with Models."

BIBLIOGRAPHY

Ackerman, James S. "Leonardo da Vinci: Art in Science." In *Science in Culture,* edited by Peter Galison, Stephen R. Graubard, and Everett Mendelsohn, 207–24. New Brunswick, NJ: Transaction, 2001.

Acland, Robert D. *Acland's Video Atlas of Human Anatomy.* 5 vols. Philadelphia, PA: Lippincott Williams and Wilkins, 2005. https://aclandanatomy.com/.

Ager, Derek. *The New Catastrophism: The Importance of the Rare Event in Geological History.* Cambridge: Cambridge University Press, 1993.

AHMM, Allies and Morrison, Aukett Swanke, BVN Architectural Services, Corstorphine + Wright, Fletcher Priest Architects, Glenn Howells Architects, Rogers, Stirk, Harbour and Partners, Zaha Hadid Architects, et al. "Open Letter to Andrew Anagnost, President and Chief Executive Officer, Autodesk." *AEC Magazine,* July 25, 2020.

Alberti, Leon Battista. *De re aedificatoria.* Florence: Nicolai Laurentii, 1485.

———. *On the Art of Building in Ten Books.* Translated by Joseph Rykwert, Neil Leach, and Robert Tavernor. Cambridge, MA: MIT Press, [1452] 1988.

Alston, George Cyprian. "Way of the Cross." In *The Catholic Encyclopedia.* New York: Robert Appleton Company, 1912.

Ambrosetti, Nadia. "Algorithmic in the 12th Century: The Carmen de Algorismo by Alexander de Villa Dei." Paper presented at HaPoC 2015 *(third international conference on History of Philosophy and Computing),* Pisa, October 2015. In *History and Philosophy of Computing: HaPoC 2015,* edited by F. Gadducci and M. Tavosanis, 71–86, IFIP Advances in Information and Communication Technology 487 (Cham, Switzerland: Springer Cham, 2016), https://doi.org/10.1007/978-3-319-47286-7_5.

Amico, Bernardino. *Plans of the Sacred Edifices of the Holy Land.* Translated by Eugene Hoade and Theophilus Bellorini. Jerusalem: Franciscan Printing Press, 1953. Translation of the original Italian *Trattato,* 1609 (1st ed.) and 1620 (2nd ed.).

———. *Trattato delle piante et imagini de i sacri edificii di Terra Santa: disegnate in Gierusalemme, secondo le regole della prospettiua, & vera misura della lor grandezza.* 1st ed. Rome: Typographia Linguarum Externarum, 1609.

———. *Trattato delle piante et imagini de i sacri edificii di Terra Santa: disegnate in Gierusalemme, secondo le regole della prospettiua, & vera misura della lor grandezza.* 2nd ed. Florence: P. Cecconcelli, 1620.

Amit, David. *Model of Jerusalem in the Second Temple Period.* Jerusalem: Israel Museum, 2009.

Anderson, William C. *A Dictionary of Law, Consisting of Judicial Definitions and Explanations of Words, Phrases, and Maxims, and an Exposition of the Principles of Law.* Union, NJ: Lawbook Exchange, [1889] 1996.

Apostel, Leo. "Towards the Formal Study of Models in the Non-Formal Sciences." In *The Concept and the Role of the Model in Mathematics and Natural and Social Sciences: Proceedings of the Colloquium Sponsored by the Division of Philosophy of Sciences of the International Union of History and Philosophy of Science Organized at Utrecht, January 1960*, edited by Hans Freudenthal, 1–37. Synthese Library. Dordrecht: Springer Netherlands, 1960.

Arata, Luis O. "A Unified View of Models." *Leonardo* 44, no. 3 (2011): 282–83.

Aristotle. *Meteorologica.* Translated by H. D. P. Lee. Loeb Classical Library 397. Cambridge, MA: Harvard University Press, [350 BCE] 1952.

Arnold, Dana. *The Spaces of the Hospital: Spatiality and Urban Change in London, 1680–1820.* Abingdon, UK: Routledge, 2013.

Atkin, Albert. "Peirce on the Index and Indexical Reference." *Transactions of the Charles S. Peirce Society* 41, no. 1 (2005): 161–88.

———. "Peirce's Theory of Signs." In *Stanford Encyclopedia of Philosophy*, edited by Edward N. Zalta. Stanford, CA: Stanford University, 2013. https://plato.stanford.edu/archives/sum2013/entries/peirce-semiotics/.

Augé, Marc. *Non-Places: Introduction to an Anthropology of Supermodernity.* Translated by John Howe. New York: Verso, 1995.

Avi-Yonah, Michael. *Pictorial Guide to the Model of Ancient Jerusalem at the Time of the Second Temple in the Grounds of the Holyland Hotel Jerusalem Israel.* Jerusalem: Holy Land Corporation, n.d. (ca. 1967).

———. *A Short Guide to the Model of Ancient Jerusalem.* Jerusalem: Ahva Press, 1966.

Avi-Yonah, Michael, and Yoram Tsafrir. *Pictorial Guide to the Model of Ancient Jerusalem at the Time of the Second Temple in the Grounds of the Holy Land Hotel Jerusalem Israel.* Herzlia, Israel: Palphot, n.d. (ca. 1983).

Baden-Fuller, Charles, and Mary S. Morgan. "Business Models as Models." *Long Range Planning* 43 (2010): 156–71.

Badiou, Alain. *The Concept of the Model: An Introduction to the Materialist Epistemology of Mathematics.* Melbourne: re.press, [1969] 2007.

Baget, Jean-François, Michel Leclère, Marie-Laure Mugnier, and Eric Salvat. "On Rules with Existential Variables: Walking the Decidability Line." *Artificial Intelligence* 175 (2011): 1620–54.

Bagatti, Bellarmino. "L'industria della madreperla a Betlemme." In *Custodia di Terra Santa 1342–1942*. Jerusalem: Tipografia dei Padri Fancescani, 1951.
Banham, Reyner. "A Black Box." *New Statesman*, October 12, 1990, 22–25.
Bar, Doron. "Recreating Jewish Sanctity in Jerusalem: Mount Zion and David's Tomb, 1948–67." *Journal of Israeli History* 23, no. 2 (2004): 260–78.
Basso, Alessandra, Chiara Lisciandra, and Caterina Marchionni. "Hypothetical Models in Social Science." In *Springer Handbook of Model-Based Science*, edited by Lorenzo Magnani and Tommaso Bertolotti, 413–33. New York: Springer, 2017.
Baudrillard, Jean. "The Precession of Simulacra." In *Art after Modernism: Essays on Rethinking Representation*, edited by Brian Wallis, 253–81. New York: Museum of Modern Art, 1984.
Bell, Charles. *The Hand: Its Mechanism and Vital Endowments, as Evincing Design*. 5th ed. Bridgewater Treatises on the Power, Wisdom, and Goodness of God as Manifested in the Creation 4. London: John Murray, 1852.
———. "Theater of Anatomy, Great Windmill Street." *Lancet* 5, no. 110 (1825): 99–102.
Bernard of Clairvaux. *La Règle du Temple*. Société de l'histoire de France 228. Edited by H. de Curzon. Paris: Librairie Renouard, 1886.
———. *The Rule of the Templars: The French Text of the Rule of the Order of the Knights Templar*. Translated and edited by J. M. Upton-Ward. Woodbridge, UK: Boydell Press, 1992.
Bernhard von Breydenbach. *Peregrinatio in terram sanctam/Die heyligne reyssen gen Jherusalem*. Mainz: Erhard Reuwich, 1486.
———. *Peregrinatio in terram sanctam: Eine Pilgerreise ins Heilige Land*. Edited by Isold Mozer. Berlin: De Gruyter, 2011.
Berner, Robert A., and Antonio C. Lasaga. "Modeling the Geochemical Carbon Cycle." *Scientific American* 260 (March 1989): 74–81.
Bevan, Andrew. "Pandora's Pithos." *History and Anthropology* 29, no. 1 (2018): 7–14.
Billings, Robert William. *Architectural Illustrations of Kettering Church, Northamptonshire*. London: Thomas and William Boone, 1843.
Binski, Paul. "London, Paris, Assisi, Rome around 1300: Questioning Art Hierarchies." In *From Minor to Major: The Minor Arts in Medieval Art History*, edited by Colum Hourihane, 3–21. Princeton, NJ: Index of Christian Art, 2012.
Black, Max. *Models and Metaphors: Studies in Language and Philosophy*. Ithaca, NY: Cornell University Press, 1962.

Black, William Henry. *A Descriptive, Analytical, and Critical Catalogue of the Mss. Bequeathed unto the University of Oxford by Elias Ashmole*. 4 vols. Oxford: Oxford University Press, 1845.

Blake, John B. "The Development of American Anatomy Acts." *Journal of Medical Education* 30, no. 8 (1955): 431–39.

Bliquez, Lawrence J., and Alexander Kazhdan. "Four Testimonia to Human Dissection in Byzantine Times." *Bulletin of the History of Medicine* 58, no. 4 (1984): 554–57.

Bonora, Valentina, Grazia Tucci, and Vincenzo Vaccaro. "3D Data Fusion and Multi-Resolution Approach for a New Survey Aimed to a Complete Model of Rucellai's Chapel by Leon Battista Alberti in Florence." Paper presented at "CIPA 2005 XX International Symposium, 26 September–1 October, 2005," Turin: CIPA, 2005. https://www.cipaheritagedocumentation.org/wp-content/uploads/2018/12/Bonora-e.a.-3D-data-fusion-and-multi-resolution-approach-for-a-new-survey-aimed-to-a-complete-model-of-Rucellai%E2%80%99s-chapel-by-Leon-Battista-Alberti.pdf.

Bourdieu, Pierre. *Distinction: A Social Critique of the Judgement of Taste*. Cambridge, MA: Harvard University Press, 1984.

Bradshaw, Peter. "Assassin's Creed Review: Michael Fassbender Game Movie Achieves Transcendental Boredom." *The Guardian*, December 19, 2016.

Braun, Emily. "The Politics of Immortality: Alberti, Florence, and the Rucellai Chapel." *Marsyas: Studies in the History of Art* 22 (1983–85): 9–17.

Brenner, Erich. "Human Body Preservation—Old and New Techniques." *Journal of Anatomy* 224, no. 3 (2014): 316–44.

Brock, C. Helen. *Dr. William Hunter's Papers and Drawings in the Hunterian Collection of Glasgow University Library: A Handlist*. Cambridge: Wellcome Unit for the History of Medicine, 1990.

Brown, Bill. "Thing Theory." *Critical Inquiry* 28, no. 1 (2001): 1–22.

Brown, Dan. *The Da Vinci Code*. New York: Doubleday, 2003.

Brubaker, Leslie. "Gifts and Prayers: The Visualization of Gift Giving in Byzantium and the Mosaics of Hagia Sophia." In *The Languages of Gift in the Early Middle Ages*, edited by Wendy Davies and Paul Fouracre, 33–61. New York: Cambridge University Press, 2010.

Brueckner, Martin, Sandy Isenstadt, and Sarah Wasserman, eds. *Modelwork: Material Culture and Modeling in the Humanities*. Minneapolis: University of Minnesota Press, 2021.

Brummitt, Jamie L. "*Protestant Relics: Religion, Objects, and the Art of Mourning in the American Republic.*" PhD diss, Duke University, 2018.

Bunge, Mario. "A General Black Box Theory." *Philosophy of Science* 30, no. 4 (1963): 346–58.

Buono, Pietro-Luciano. "Models of Central Pattern Generators for Quadruped Locomotion: Secondary Gaits." *Journal of Mathematical Biology* 42 (2001): 327–46.

Burckhardt, Jacob. *The Civilization of the Renaissance in Italy*. Edited by S. G. C. Middlemore. London: George Allen and Unwin, [1860] 1878.

"Burial." At Body Donation resource page, website of Sackler Faculty of Medicine, Tel Aviv University, n.d. https://en-med.tau.ac.il/Procedure-for-the-reception-and-transfer-of-a-body/?tab=4.

Butler, Alan, and Stephen Dafoe. *The Warriors and the Bankers: A History of the Knights Templar from 1307 to the Present*. Belleville, ONT: Templar Books, 1998.

Bynum, Caroline Walker. *Fragmentation and Redemption: Essays on Gender and the Human Body in Medieval Religion*. New York: Zone Books, 1991.

Camille, Michael. "Simulacrum." In *Critical Terms for Art History*, edited by Robert S. Nelson and Richard Shiff, 31–44. Chicago: University of Chicago Press, 2003.

Campbell, Mungo, and Nathan Flis, eds. *William Hunter and the Anatomy of the Modern Museum*. New Haven, CT: Yale Center for British Art, 2018.

Carpo, Mario. *The Alphabet and the Algorithm*. Cambridge, MA: MIT Press, 2011.

———. *Architecture in the Age of Printing: Orality, Writing, Typography, and Printed Images in the History of Architectural Theory*. Translated by Sarah Benson. Cambridge, MA: MIT Press, 2001.

———. *The Second Digital Turn: Design beyond Intelligence*. Writing Architecture. Edited by Cynthia Davidson. Cambridge, MA: MIT Press, 2017.

Cartwright, Nancy. "Scientific Models Versus Social Reality." *Building Research and Information* 44, no. 3 (2015): 334–37.

Casti, John L. *Alternate Realities: Mathematical Models of Nature and Man*. New York: Wiley, 1989.

Celsus, Aulus Cornelius. *On Medicine [De medicina]*. 3 vols. Translated by W. G. Spencer. Loeb Classical Library 292. London: William Heinemann, [1st cent. CE] 1935.

Champney, Thomas. "The Business of Bodies: Ethical Perspectives on For-Profit Body Donation Companies." *Clinical Anatomy* 29, no. 1 (2016): 25–29.

Chaney, Annie. *Body Brokers: Inside America's Underground Trade in Human Remains*. New York: Random House, 2007.

Chang, C. C., and H. Jerome Keisler. *Model Theory.* Chicago: Dover, 2012.
Chaplain of Sir Richard Guylforde. *Pylgrymage of Sir Richard Guylforde to the Holy Land, A.D. 1506.* Edited by Henry Ellis. London: J. B. Nichols and Son, 1851.
Chaplin, Simon. "Anatomy and the 'Museum Oeconomy': William and John Hunter as Collectors." In *William Hunter's World: The Art and Science of Eighteenth-Century Collecting,* edited by E. Geoffrey Hancock, Nick Pearce, and Mungo Campbell, 45–58. Histories of Material Culture and Collecting, 1700–1950. Farnham, UK: Ashgate, 2015.
Charlier, Philippe, et al. "A Glimpse into the Early Origins of Medieval Anatomy through the Oldest Conserved Human Dissection (Western Europe, 13th c. C.E.)." *Archives of Medical Science* 10, no. 2 (2014): 366–73.
Cheeseman, James F., Craig D. Millar, Uwe Greggers, Konstantin Lehmann, Matthew D. M. Pawley, Charles R. Gallistel, Guy R. Warman, and Randolf Manzel. "Way-Finding in Displaced Clock-Shifted Bees Proves Bees Use a Cognitive Map." *Proceedings of the National Academy of Science* 111, no. 24 (2014): 8949–54.
Choulant, Ludwig. *History and Bibliography of Anatomic Illustration.* Translated by Mortimer Frank. New York: Hafner, [1852] 1962.
Chung, Beom Sun, Koojoo Kwon, Byeong-Seok Shin, and Min Suk Chung. "Peeled and Piled Volume Models of the Stomach Made from a Cadaver's Sectioned Images." *International Journal of Morphology* 34, no. 3 (2016): 939–44.
Church of England. *Liturgies and Occasional Forms of Prayer Set Forth in the Reign of Queen Elizabeth.* Cambridge: Cambridge University Press, 1847.
Clarke, Kevin A., and David M. Primo. *A Model Discipline: Political Science and the Logic of Representations.* Oxford: Oxford University Press, 2012.
Collin, Robbie. "Assassin's Creed Review: Even Michael Fassbender Can't Make This Junk Leap Off the Screen." *Daily Telegraph,* December 19, 2016.
Collinge, William H. "Exploring Construction Project Design as Multimodal Social Semiotic Practice." *Social Semiotics* 29, no. 5 (2019): 603–21.
Collyer, Charles E. "Notes and Comment: Comparing Strong and Weak Models by Fitting Them to Computer-Generated Data." *Perception and Psychophysics* 38, no. 5 (1985): 476–81.
Conder, Charles Reignier. *Tent Work in Palestine: A Record of Discovery and Adventure.* 2 vols. Vol. 2. London: Richard Bentley & Son, 1879.
Contessa, Gabriele. "Scientific Models and Representation." In *The Continuum Companion to the Philosophy of Science,* edited by Steven French and Juha Saatsi, 120–35. New York: Continuum, 2011.

Cornwall, Jon, Gary F. Perry, Graham Louw, and Mark D. Stringer. "Who Donates Their Body to Science? An International, Multicenter, Prospective Study." *Anatomical Sciences Education* 5 (2012): 208–16.

Crutzen, Paul J. "Geology of Mankind." *Nature* 415 (January 3, 2002): 23.

Curzon, Henri de. *La maison du temple de Paris, histoire et description*. Paris: Librairie Hachette, 1888.

Cust, L. G. A. *The Status Quo in the Holy Places*. Jerusalem: Ariel, [1929] 1980.

Dalman, Gustaf. "Die Modelle der Grabeskirche und Grabeskapelle in Jerusalem als Quelle ihrer älteren Gestalt." *Palästinajahrbuch des Deutschen evangelischen Instituts für Altertumswissenschaft des Heiligen Landes zu Jerusalem* 16 (1920): 23–31.

Daston, Lorraine, and Peter Galison. *Objectivity*. Cambridge, MA: Zone Books, 2007.

Davies, Jeremy. *The Birth of the Anthropocene*. Oakland: University of California Press, 2016.

Davis, Daniel. "Architects versus Autodesk." Website of the Journal of the American Institute of Architects, August 27, 2020. https://www.architect magazine.com/technology/architects-versus-autodesk_o.

de Certeau, Michel. *The Practice of Everyday Life*. Translated by Steven F. Rendall. Berkeley: University of California Press, 1984.

de Klerck, Brum. "Jerusalem in Renaissance Italy." In *The Imagined and Real Jerusalem in Art and Architecture*, edited by Jeroen Goudeau, Mariëtte Verhoeven, and Wouter Weijers, 215–36. Radboud Studies in Humanities. Leiden: Brill, 2014.

de Sacy, Silvestre. "Mémoire sur la dynastie des Assassins, et sur l' étymologie de leur Nom." *Mémoires de l'Istitut Royal de France* 4 (1818): 1–84.

Dee, M. I. [John]. "Preface." In *Euclid's Elements of Geometry. Faithfully (now first) translated into the Englishe toung, by H. Billingsley, citizen of London. Whereunto are annexed certaine scholies, annotations, and inuentions, of the best mathematiciens, both of time past, and in this our age. With a very fruitfull praeface made by M. I. Dee, specifying the chiefe mathematicall scie[n]ces, what they are, and wherunto commodious: where, also, are disclosed certaine new secrets mathematicall and mechanicall, vntill these our daies, greatly missed*. 1570.

Dejure, Antonella. "La 'Legenda' volgare di santa Chiara da Montefalco: tradizione manocritta e appunti linguistici." *Archivum Franciscanum Historicum* 103 (July–December 2010): 423–70.

Delisle, Léopold. *Mémoire sur les opérations financières des Templiers.* Vol. 33, pt. 2. Paris: Académie des inscriptions et belles-lettres, 1889. Geneva: Slatkine-Megariotis Reprints, 1975.

Der Bedrosian, Jeanette. "First-Year Medical Students Still Rely on Cadavers to Learn Anatomy." *Johns Hopkins Magazine,* Winter 2016, 1–10.

Descartes, René. *Discours de la methode pour bien conduire sa raison & chercher la verité dans les sciences plus la dioptrique, les meteores, et la geometrie.* Leiden: Ian Maire, 1637.

Désilets, Patrice. "Assassin's Creed." Montreal: Ubisoft, 2007.

Dessi Bardeschi, Marco. "Nuove ricerche sul S. Sepolcro nella Cappella Rucellai a Firenze." *Marmo* 2 (1963): 135–61.

Dondi, Cristina. *The Liturgy of the Canons Regular of the Holy Sepulchre of Jerusalem: A Study and a Catalogue of the Manuscript Sources.* Bibliotheca Victorina 16. Turnhout, Belgium: Brepols, 2004.

Dove, W. "The Temple Church and Its Restoration." *Transactions of the London and Middlesex Archeological Society* (1967): 164–72.

Echenique, Marcial. "Models: A Discussion." *Journal of Architectural Research* 1, no. 1 (1970): 25–30.

Eckert, W. J., and Rebecca Bradley Jones. *Faster, Faster: A Simple Description of a Giant Electronic Calculator and the Problems It Solves.* New York: McGraw-Hill, 1955.

Edwards, Paul N. *A Vast Machine: Computer Models, Climate Data, and the Politics of Global Warming.* Cambridge, MA: MIT Press, 2010.

Eisenman, Peter, Richard Pommer, and Christian Hubert. *Idea as Model.* New York: Rizzoli, 1981.

Eisenstein, Elizabeth. *The Printing Revolution in Early Modern Europe.* 2nd ed. Cambridge: Cambridge University Press, 2005.

Encyclopedia of Business. "Models and Modeling." Encyclopedia of Business in *Reference for Business.* Advameg, Inc., 2013. http://www.referenceforbusiness.com/management/Mar-No/Models-and-Modeling.html.

Erasmus, Desiderius. *Adages.* Translated by Margaret Mann Phillips. Vol. 31 of *Collected Works of Erasmus,* 85 vols. Toronto: University of Toronto Press, 1974.

———. *Adagia chiliades.* Tubingen: In ædibus Thomæ Anshelmi Badensis, 1514. https://books.google.com/books?id=UfBSAAAAcAAJ&printsec=frontcover&source=gbs_ge_summary_r&cad=0#v=onepage&q=Hostium%20munera%20non%20munera&f=false.

———. *Colloquies: A Pilgrimage for Religion's Sake*. Edited by Craig R. Thompson. Vol. 40 of *Collected Works of Erasmus*. 85 vols. Toronto: University of Toronto Press, [1518] 1997.

European Centre for Medium-Range Weather Forecasts. "ECMWF Home." 2018. https://www.ecmwf.int/.

Fabricius, Johann C. *Briefe aus London vermischten Inhalts*. Dessau: Buchhandlung der Gelehrten, 1784.

Fagan, Madeleine. "On the Dangers of an Anthropocene Epoch: Geological Time, Political Time and Post-Human Politics." *Political Geography* 70 (2019): 55–63.

Farahani, Navid, Alex Braun, Dylan Jutt, Todd Huffman, Nick Reder, Zheng Liu, Yukako Yagi, and Liron Pantanowitz. "Three-dimensional Imaging and Scanning: Current and Future Applications for Pathology." *Journal of Pathology Informatics* 8, no. 36 (2017): n.p.

Farre, John. "Advertisement for Morbid Anatomy." *Medico-Chirurgical Review*, n.s., 6, no. 10 (April 1827): 630–32.

Feinstein, Stephen C. "Zbigniew Libera's Lego Concentration Camp: Iconoclasm in Conceptual Art about the Shoah." *Other Voices* 2, no. 1 (2000): n.p.

Ferckel, Christoph. "Weitere Beiträge zur Geschichte der Anatomie im Mittelalter." *Archiv für Geschichte der Medizin* 10, no. 5 (1917): 255–63.

Ferrari, Giovanna. "Public Anatomy Lessons and the Carnival: The Anatomy Theatre of Bologna." *Past and Present* 117 (1987): 50–106.

Ferri, Rick. "The Curse of the Yale Model." *Forbes Online*, April 16, 2012. https://www.forbes.com/sites/rickferri/2012/04/16/the-curse-of-the-yale-model/#7cb8bd03dae9.

Finucci, Valeria, and Maurizio Rippa Bonati, eds. "Vesalius and the Languages of Anatomy." Special issue, *Journal of Medieval and Early Modern Studies* 48, no. 1 (2018).

"First Day in Gross Anatomy Lab." Duke University Medical Center, 2013.

Fleck, Ludwik. *Genesis and Development of a Scientific Fact*. Translated by Frederick Bradley and Taddeus J. Trenn. Chicago: University of Chicago Press, [1935] 1981.

Folda, Jaroslav. *The Art of the Crusaders in the Holy Land, 1098–1187*. Cambridge: Cambridge University Press, 1995.

Foucault, Michel. *Discipline and Punish: The Birth of the Prison*. Translated by A. Sheridan. New York: Random House, [1975] 1979.

Frankfurt, Harry G. *On Bullshit*. Princeton, NJ: Princeton University Press, 2005.

Frigg, Roman. "Models and Fiction." *Synthese* 172, no. 1 (2010): 251–68.
Frigg, Roman, and Stephan Hartmann. "Models in Science." In *The Stanford Encyclopedia of Philosophy*, edited by Edward N. Zalta. Stanford, CA: Stanford University Press, 2012. http://plato.stanford.edu/entries/models-science/.
Gamer, Meredith. "Scalpel to Burin: A Material History of William Hunter's Anatomy of the Human Gravid Uterus." In *William Hunter and the Anatomy of the Modern Museum*, edited by Mungo Campbell and Nathan Flis, 108–25. New Haven, CT: Yale Center for British Art, 2018.
Gannal, Jean-Nicolas. *History of Embalming and of Preparation in Anatomy, Pathology, and Natural History*. Translated by R. Harlan. Philadelphia: Judah Dobson, 1840.
Garment, Ann, Susan Lederer, Naomi Rogers, and Lisa Boult. "Let the Dead Teach the Living: The Rise of Body Bequeathal in 20th-Century America." *Academic Medicine* 82, no. 10 (2007): 1000–1005.
Geertz, Clifford. "Religion as a Cultural System." In *The Interpretation of Cultures: Selected Essays*, 87–125. London: Fontana Press, [1973] 1993.
Gelfert, Axel. *How to Do Science with Models: A Philosophical Primer*. New York: Springer, 2016.
———. "The Ontology of Models." In *Springer Handbook of Model-Based Science*, edited by Lorenzo Magnani and Tommaso Bertolotti, 5–23. New York: Springer, 2017.
Giannopoulou, Mimika. *Pithoi: Technology and History of Storage Vessels through the Ages*. Oxford: Archaeopress Publishing, 2011.
Gibbard, Allan, and Hal R. Varian. "Economic Models." *Journal of Philosophy* 75, no. 11 (1978): 664–77.
Gieben, Servus. *Lo stemma francescano: Origine e sviluppo*. Iconographia Francescana 18. Rome: Istituto Storico dei Cappuccini, 2009.
Giere, Ronald N. "How Models Are Used to Represent Reality." In "Proceedings of the 2002 Biennial Meeting of The Philosophy of Science Association. Part II: Symposia Papers," edited by Sandra D. Mitchell, *Philosophy of Science* 71, no. 5 (2004): 742–52.
Godfrey, Walter Hinds. "Recent Discoveries at the Temple, London, and Notes on the Topography of the Site." *Archaeologia: Miscellaneous Tracts Relating to Antiquity* 95 (1953): 123–40.
Goldstein, Hilary. "Assassin's Creed Review." IGN, November 13, 2007. https://www.ign.com/articles/2007/11/13/assassins-creed-review.
Goodman, Nelson. *Languages of Art: An Approach to a Theory of Symbols*. Indianapolis, IN: Hackett, [1976] 1985.

Gordon, Charles George. *Reflections in Palestine.* London: Macmillan, 1884.
Graciano, Andrew, ed. *Visualizing the Body in Art, Anatomy, and Medicine since 1800: Models and Modeling.* Science and the Arts since 1750. London: Routledge, 2019.
Green, Monica H. "From 'Diseases of Women' to 'Secrets of Women': The Transformation of Gynecological Literature in the Later Middle Ages." *Journal of Medieval and Early Modern Studies* 30, no. 1 (2000): 5–39.
Gurdasani, Deepti, and Hisham Ziauddeen. "On the Fallibility of Simulation Models in Informing Pandemic Responses." *Lancet* 8 (2020): 776–77.
Hall, Dominic William. "The Catholic Brahmin and the Anatomy Act of 1898: Thomas Dwight and the Normalization of the Medical Cadaver Supply in Late Nineteenth-Century Massachusetts." MA thesis, Harvard University, 2018.
Hall, Stuart. *Representation: Cultural Representations and Signifying Practices.* London: Sage, 1997.
Halperin, Edward C. "The Poor, the Black, and the Marginalized as the Source of Cadavers in United States Anatomical Education." *Clinical Anatomy* 20, no. 5 (2007): 489–95.
Handerson, Henry E. *Gilbertus Anglicus: Medicine of the Thirteenth Century.* Cleveland, OH: Cleveland Medical Library Association, 1918.
Harcourt, Glenn. "Andreas Vesalius and the Anatomy of Antique Sculpture." *Representations* 17 (Winter 1987): 28–61.
Harrison, Jane E. "Pandora's Box." *Journal of Hellenic Studies* 20 (1900): 99–114.
"Has Our Climate Changed?" *Scientific American* 28, no. 20 (1872): 305.
Haselberger, Lothar. "Architectural Likenesses: Models and Plans of Architecture." *Journal of Roman Studies* 10 (1997): 77–94.
Hasselquist, Fredrik. *Voyages and Travels in the Levant in the Years 1749–1752.* London: L. Davis and C. Reymers, 1766.
Haugeland, John. "Analog and Analog." *Philosophical Topics* 12, no. 1 (1981): 213–25.
Hayashi, Shogo, Munekazo Naito, Shinichi Kawata, and Ning Qu. "History and Future of Cadaver Preservation for Surgical Training: From Formalin to Saturated Salt Solution Method." *Anatomy Research International* 91 (2016): 1–7.
Hayles, N. Katherine. *How We Became Posthuman: Virtual Bodies in Cybernetics, Literature, and Informatics.* Chicago: University of Chicago Press, 1999.
Hellewell, Joel, Sebastian Funk, and Rosalind M. Eggo. "On the Fallibility of Simulation Models in Informing Pandemic Responses: Authors' Reply." *Lancet* 8 (2020): 778.

Henry, Brandon Michael, Jens Vikse, Przemyslaw Pekala, Marios Loukas, R. Shane Tubbs, Jerzy A. Walocha, D. Gareth Jones, and Krzysztof A. Tomaszewski. "Consensus Guidelines for the Uniform Reporting of Study Ethics in Anatomical Research within the Framework of the Anatomical Quality Assurance (AQUA) Checklist." *Clinical Anatomy 31* (2018): 521–24.

Heseler, Baldasar. *Andreas Vesalius' First Public Anatomy at Bologna, 1540: An Eyewitness Report by Baldasar Heseler Together with His Notes on Matthaeus Curtius' Lectures on Anatomia Mundini*. Translated by Ruben Eriksson. Uppsala: Almquist and Wiksells, [1540] 1959.

Hesiod. *Theogony, Works and Days, Testimonia*. Vol. 1. Edited and translated by Glenn W. Most. Loeb Classical Library 57. Cambridge, MA: Harvard University Press, 1950.

Heydenreich, Ludwig H. "Die Cappella Rucellai von San Pancrazio in Florence." In *De Artibus Opuscula XL: Essays in Honor of Erwin Panofsky*, edited by Millard Meiss, 219–29. New York: New York University Press, 1961.

Hick, W. E. "The Impact of Information Theory on Psychology." *Advancement of Science (Symposium on Cybernetics)* 40 (March 1954): 397–402.

Hochfelder, David. *The Telegraph in America, 1832–1920*. Baltimore, MD: John Hopkins University Press, 2012.

Huizinga, Johan. *Homo Ludens: A Study of the Play Element in Culture*. New York: Roy Publishers, [1938] 1950.

Hulme, Mike. "How Climate Models Gain and Exercise Authority." In *The Social Life of Climate Change Models*, edited by Kirsten Hastrup and Martin Skrydstrup, 30–44. Routledge Studies in Anthropology. New York: Routledge, 2013.

Hummel, Daniel G. "His Land and the Origins of the Jewish-Evangelical Israel Lobby." *Church History* 87, no. 4 (2018): 1119–51.

Hunter, William. *Anatomia uteri humani gravidi tabulis illustrata*. Birmingham and London: S. Baker, T. Cadell, D. Wilson, T. Nichol, and J. Murray, 1774.

———. *Dr. William Hunter at the Royal Academy of Arts*. Glasgow: Glasgow University Press, [1769–72] 1975.

———. *Two Introductory Lectures Delivered by Dr. William Hunter, to his Last Course of Anatomical Lectures, at his Theatre in Windmill-Street*. London: J. Johnson, 1784.

———. "Will of William Hunter, Doctor in Physic of Windmill Street Westminster, Middlesex." April 4, 1783. Held at The National Archives, Kew, Prerogative Court of Canterbury, Wills and Probate, PROB 11/1102/94.

Idso, Craig D., Robert M. Carter, and S. Fred Singer. *Why Scientists Disagree about Global Warming: The NIPCC Report on Scientific Consensus*. 2nd ed. Nongovernmental International Panel on Climate Change. Arlington Heights, IL: Heartland Institute, 2016.

Impey, Oliver, and Arthur MacGregor, eds. *The Origins of Museums: The Cabinets of Curiosities in Sixteenth- and Seventeenth-Century Europe.* 2nd ed. Oxford: Ashmolean, 2017.

Ivins, William M. "A Propos of the 'Fabrica' of Vesalius." *Bulletin of the History of Medicine* 14 (January 1943): 576–93.

———. "What about the 'Fabrica' of Vesalius?'" In *Three Vesalian Essays to Accompany the "Icones Anatomicae" of 1934*, edited by Samuel W. Lambert, Willy Wiegand, and William M. Ivins, 43–99. History of Medicine Series of the Library of the New York Academy of Medicine. New York: MacMillan, 1952.

Izzett, David S. T., W. L. White, and W. S. Hardcastle. *The Garden Tomb Jerusalem.* London: Committee of the Garden Tomb [Jerusalem] Association, 1967.

Jackson, Kerry. "The Truth Warming Alarmists Don't Want You to Know about the Climate Models." *Investor's Business Daily,* May 25, 2016.

Jagadheeswari, R., R. Gayatri Devi, and A. Jothi Priya. "Evaluating the Effects of Video Games on Blood Pressure and Heart Rate." *Drug Invention Today* 10, no. 1 (2018): 2702–4.

Jameson, Fredric. *Postmodernism: The Cultural Logic of Late Capitalism.* Durham, NC: Duke University Press, 1990.

Jebeile, Julie, and Ashley Graham Kennedy. "Explaining with Models: The Role of Idealizations." *International Studies in the Philosophy of Science* 29, no. 4 (2015): 383–92.

Jenkins, George B. "The Legal Status of Dissecting. From the Anatomical Laboratory of Johns Hopkins University." *Anatomical Record* 7, no. 11 (1913): 387–99.

Jewitt, Dave. "Accuracy vs. Authenticity in Video Games." YouTube, April 3, 2018. https://www.youtube.com/watch?v=y73HFDnUOJo.

Johnson, Samuel. *Notes to Shakespeare, Volume III: The Tragedies.* Gutenberg Project, [1765] 1958. https://www.gutenberg.org/files/15566/15566.txt.

Jones, D. Gareth. "Bioethical Aspects of Commemorations and Memorials." In *Commemorations and Memorials: Exploring the Human Face of Anatomy,* edited by Goran Strkalj and Nalini Pather, 15–26. Singapore: World Scientific Publishing, 2017.

Jones, Peter Murray. "Image, Word and Medicine in the Middle Ages." In *Visualizing Medieval Medicine and Natural History, 1200–1550,* edited by Jean A.

Givens, Karen M. Reeds, and Alain Touwaide, 1–24. AVISTA Studies in the History of Medieval Technology, Science and Art. Aldershot, UK: Ashgate, 2006.

Jordanova, Ludmilla. "Gender, Generation, and Science: William Hunter's Obstetrical Atlas." In *William Hunter and the Eighteenth-Century Medical World*, edited by W. F. Bynum and Roy Porter, 385–412. Cambridge: Cambridge University Press, 1985.

———. "Material Models as Visual Culture." In *Models: The Third Dimension of Science*, edited by Soraya de Chadarevian and Nick Hopwood, 443–51. Stanford, CA: Stanford University Press, 2004.

Jotischky, Andrew. "The Franciscan Return to the Holy Land (1333) and Mt. Sion Pilgrimage and the Apostolic Mission." In *The Crusader World*, edited by Adrian J. Boas, 241–55. London: Routledge, 2016.

Kalanithi, Paul. *When Breath Becomes Air*. London: Vintage Books, 2017.

Kemp, Martin. "A Drawing for the 'Fabrica': and Some Thoughts upon the Vesalius Muscle-men." *Medical History* 14, no. 3 (1970): 277–88.

———. *Leonardo*. Oxford: Oxford University Press, 2011.

———. "True to Their Natures: Sir Joshua Reynolds and Dr. William Hunter at the Royal Academy of the Arts." *Royal Society Journal of the History of Science* 46, no. 1 (1992): 77–88.

Kemp, Martin, and Marina Wallace. *Spectacular Bodies: The Art and Science of the Human Body from Leonardo to Now*. Berkeley: Hayward Gallery and University of California Press, 2000.

Kempe, Margery. *The Book of Margery Kempe*. Edited by Anthony Bale. Oxford World's Classics. Oxford: Oxford University Press, 2015.

Kent, Francis William. "The Letters Genuine and Spurious of Giovanni Rucellai." *Journal of the Warburg and Courtauld Institutes* 37 (1974): 342–49.

———. "The Making of a Renaissance Patron of the Arts." In *Giovanni Rucellai ed il suo "Zibaldone," vol. 2, A Florentine Patrician and His Palace*, introduction by Nicolai Rubinstein. Studies of the Warburg Institute 24, 9–95. London: Warburg Institute, University of London, 1981.

Kim, Jeffrey. "A Pilot of Student-Guided Virtual Reality Tours." In *CITC Global*, 1–8. London: Springer, 2019.

King, Helen. "History without Historians? Medical History and the Internet." *Social History of Medicine* 24, no. 2 (2012): 212–21.

Kirkpatrick, David D., Matt Apuzzo, and Selam Gebrekidan. "Europe Said It Was Pandemic-Ready: Pride Was Its Downfall." *New York Times*, July 20, 2020.

Klinkenberg, Emanuel S. *Compressed Meanings: The Donor's Model in Medieval Art to around 1300: Origin, Spread and Significance of an Architectural Image in the Realm of Tension between Tradition and Likeness*. Architectura Medii Aevi. Edited by Thomas Coomans Turnhout: Brepols, 2009.

Knyveton, John. *Man Midwife: The Further Experiences of John Knyveton, M.D.* London: Hale, [1809] 1946.

Krämer, Michael. "The Philosophy of the Large Hadron Collider." *The Guardian*, June 6, 2015.

Krautheimer, Richard. "Commentary on Heydenreich's observations in 'Die Cappella Rucellai und die Badia Fiesolana. Untersuchung über architektonische Stilformen Albertis.'" *Kunstchronik* 13, no. 12 (1960): 353–54.

——. "Introduction to an 'Iconography of Medieval Architecture.'" *Journal of the Warburg and Courtauld Institutes* 5 (1942): 1–33.

Kuo, Andrew, Jacob L. Hiler, and Richard J. Lutz. "From Super Mario to Skyrim: A Framework for the Evolution of Video Game Consumption." *Journal of Consumer Behavior* 16, no. 2 (2016): 101–20.

Kusukawa, Sachiko. *Picturing the Book of Nature: Image, Text, and Argument in Sixteenth-Century Human Anatomy and Medical Botany*. Chicago: University of Chicago Press, 2012.

Lambert, Samuel W. "The Initial Letters of the Anatomical Treatise, *De Humani Corporis Fabrica*, of Vesalius." In *Three Vesalian Essays to Accompany the "Icones Anatomicae" of 1934*, edited by Samuel W. Lambert, Willy Wiegand, and William M. Ivins, 1–24. History of Medicine Series of the Library of the New York Academy of Medicine. New York: MacMillan, 1952.

Latour, Bruno. *Reassembling the Social: An Introduction to Actor-Network-Theory*. Clarendon Lectures in Management Studies. Oxford: Oxford University Press, 2005.

——. *Science in Action: How to Follow Scientists and Engineers through Society*. Cambridge, MA: Harvard University Press, 1987.

——. "Visualization and Cognition." *Knowledge and Society* 6 (1986): 1–40.

——. *We Have Never Been Modern*. Translated by Catherine Porter. Cambridge, MA: Harvard University Press, 1993.

Latour, Bruno, and Steve Woolgar. *Laboratory Life: The Construction of Scientific Facts*. Princeton, NJ: Princeton University Press, [1979] 1986.

Law, Jonathan, and Elizabeth A. Martin. "A Dictionary of Law." *Oxford Reference Online*, Oxford University Press, 2009, 2013. http://www.oxfordreference.com.proxy.lib.duke.edu/view/10.1093/acref/9780199551248.001.0001/acref-9780199551248-e-144?rskey=0ykrwp&result=160&q=.

Le Goff, Jacques. *Must We Divide History into Periods?* Edited by M. B. DeBevoise. New York: Columbia University Press, 2015.

Lemmens, Leonardus. *Acta S. Congregationis de Propaganda Fide pro Terra Sancta (Paris I, 1622–1720)*. Biblioteca Bio-Bibliografica. Edited by Girolamo Golubovic. Nuova serie—documenti 3, pars 1. Florence: Collegio di S. Bonaventura, 1921.

Lernout, Geert. "The Angel of Philology." *European Studies* 26 (2008): 45–61.

Leslie, Fiona. "Inside Outside: Changing Attitudes towards Architectural Models in the Museum at South Kensington." *Architectural History: Journal of the Society of Architectural Historians of Great Britain* 47 (2004): 150–200.

Levins, Richard. "The Strategy of Model Building in Population Biology." *American Scientist* 54, no. 4 (1966): 421–31.

Levy, Arnon. "Fictional Models *de novo* and *de re*." PhilSci Archive, University of Pittsburgh, 2012. http://philsci-archive.pitt.edu/9075/.

Lewer, David, and Robert Dark. *The Temple Church in London*. London: Historical Publications, 1997.

Linder, Amnon. "The Liturgy of the Liberation of Jerusalem." *Medieval Studies* 52 (1990): 110–31.

Log. Special issue, "Model Behavior." 50 (2020).

Lutz, Arthur F., Herbert W. ter Maat, Hester Biemans, Arun B. Shrestha, Philippus Wester, and Walter W. Immerzeel. "Selecting Representative Climate Models for Climate Change Impact Studies: An Advanced Envelope-Based Selection Approach." *International Journal of Climatology* 36 (2016): 3988–4005.

MacDonald, Helen. *Human Remains: Dissection and Its Histories*. New Haven, CT: Yale University Press, 2006.

MacKay, Donald M. "Towards an Information-Flow Model of Human Behaviour." *British Journal of Psychology* 47, no. 1 (1956): 30–43.

MacKie, E. W. "William Hunter and Captain Cook: The 18th Century Ethnographical Collection in the Hunterian Museum." *Glasgow Archaeological Journal* 12 (1985): 1–18.

MacKinney, L. C., and Harry Bober. "A Thirteenth-Century Medical Case History in Miniatures, with a Stylistic Analysis of the Miniatures by Harry Bober." *Speculum* 35, no. 2 (1960): 251–59.

Magnani, Lorenzo, and Tommaso Bertolotti, eds. *Springer Handbook of Model-Based Science*. New York: Springer, 2017.

Magni, Cornelio. *Quanto di più curioso e vago ha potuto vedere Cornelio Magna*. Parma: Alberto Pazzoni and Paolo Monti, 1692.

Mäki, Uskali. "Models and the Locus of Their Truth." *Synthese* 180 (2011): 47–63.
Marmoy, C. F. A. "The 'Auto-Icon' of Jeremy Bentham at University College London." *Medical History* 2 (1958): 77–86.
Martin, James. "A Christian Hurricane Prayer." HuffPost, December 29, 2012. https://www.huffingtonpost.com/rev-james-martin-sj/a-hurricane-prayer_b_2038613.html.
Martin, Marcus L., and Kirt von Daacke. "President's Commission on Slavery and the University: Report to President Teresa A. Sullivan." Charlottesville: University of Virginia, 2018. http://vpdiversity.virginia.edu/sites/vpdiversity.virginia.edu/files/PCSU%20Report%20FINAL_July%202018.pdf.
Mason, Carol I. "Reading the Rings: Decoding Iconographic ('Jesuit') Rings." *Historical Archaeology* 44, no. 2 (2010): 8–13.
Mayo Clinic. "Body Donation at Mayo Clinic: Why a Donation May Be Denied." 1998–. https://www.mayoclinic.org/body-donation/why-donation-denied.
Mazzotti, Giovanni, Mirella Falconi, Gabriella Teti, Michela Zago, and Marcello Lanari. "The Diagnosis of the Cause of the Death of Venerina." *Journal of Anatomy* 216 (2010): 271–74.
McCall, Taylor. "Reliquam dicit pictura: Text and Image in a Twelfth-Century Illustrated Anatomical Manual (Gonville and Caius College, Cambridge, MS 190/223)." *Transactions of the Cambridge Bibliographical Society* 16, no. 1 (2016): 1–22.
McCarty, Willard. "Modeling: A Study in Words and Meanings." In *A Companion to Digital Humanities*, edited by Susan Schreibman, Ray Siemens, and John Unsworth. Oxford: Blackwell, 2004.
McCormack, Helen. "Housing the Collection: The Great Windmill Street Anatomy Theatre and Museum." In *"My highest pleasures": William Hunter's Art Collection*, edited by Peter Black. Glasgow: University of Glasgow Press, 2007.
McCracken-Flesher, Caroline. *The Doctor Dissected: A Cultural Autopsy of the Burke and Hare Murders*. Oxford: Oxford University Press, 2012.
McCulloch, N. A., D. Russell, and Stuart W. McDonald. "William Hunter's Gravid Uterus: The Specimens and Plates." *Clinical Anatomy* 15 (2002): 253–62.
McDonald, Stuart W., and John W. Faithfull. "William Hunter's Sources of Pathological and Anatomical Specimens, with Particular Reference to Obstetric Subjects." In *William Hunter's World: The Art and Science of Eighteenth-Century Collecting*, edited by E. Geoffrey Hancock, Nick Pearce, and Mungo Campbell. Farnham, UK: Ashgate, 2015.

McIsaac, Peter M. "Gunther von Hagens' Body Worlds: Exhibitionary Practice, German History and Difference." In *Museums and Difference*, edited by Daniel J. Sherman, 155–202. Bloomington: Indiana University Press, 2007.

McKitterick, David. *Print, Manuscript and the Search for Order, 1450–1830*. Cambridge: Cambridge University Press, 2005.

McMahn, Alison. "Immersion, Engagement, and Presence: A Method for Analyzing 3-D Video Games." In *The Video Game Theory Reader*, edited by Mark J. P. Wolf and Bernard Perron, 67–86. New York: Routledge, 2003.

McMahon, Tony. "British Museum Takes Apart 1600s Model of the Holy Sepulchre." YouTube, April 8, 2012. https://www.youtube.com/watch?v=vmhhJdnAXZo.

McPartland, Richard. "BIM Dimensions—3D, 4D, 5D, 6D BIM Explained." NBS Enterprises. https://www.thenbs.com/knowledge/bim-dimensions-3d-4d-5d-6d-bim-explained.

Mele, Caterina. "Il Sacello del Santo Sepolcro nella Cappella Rucellai." In *Postgotico e Rinascimento*, edited by Giuseppe Rocchi Coopmans de Yoldi, 209–31. Florence: Alinea, 2002.

Meli, Domenico Bertoloni. *Visualizing Disease: The Art and History of Pathological Illustrations*. Chicago: University of Chicago Press, 2017.

Menestò, Enrico. "Il processo apostolico per la canonizzazione di Chiara da Montefalco (1318–1319)." In *S. Chiara da Montefalco e il suo tempo: Atti del quarto Convegno di studi storici ecclesiastici organizzato dall'Archidiocesi di Spoleto, Spoleto, 28–30 dicembre 1981: Il processo di canonizzazione di Chiara da Montefalco*, edited by Claudio Leonardi and Enrico Menestò. Quaderni del Centro per il Collegamento degli Studi Medievali e Umanistici nell'Universtà di Perugia, 269–301. Florence: Nuova Italia, 1984.

Merrigan, Thomas D. "Anatomy." In *Catholic Encyclopedia*, edited by Charles G. Herbermann, 457–61. New York: Robert Appleton Company, 1907.

Metcalf, D. M. "The Templars as Bankers and Monetary Transfers between West and East in the Twelfth Century." In *Coinage in the Latin East*, edited by P. W. Edbury and D. M. Metcalf, 1–17. BAR International Series 77. Oxford: BAR, 1980.

Meyers, Carol L. "Temple, Jerusalem." In *Anchor Bible Dictionary*, edited by David Noel Freedman, 350–69. New York: Doubleday, 1992.

Michaels, Patrick J., and David E. Wojick. "Climate Modeling Dominates Climate Science." Washington, DC: Cato Institute, May 13, 2016. https://www.cato.org/blog/climate-modeling-dominates-climate-science.

Mitchell, Piers, ed. *Anatomical Dissection in Enlightenment England and Beyond: Autopsy, Pathology and Display*. London: Routledge, 2012.

Michelson, Emily. "Bernardino of Siena Visualizes the Name of God." In *Speculum Sermonis: Interdisciplinary Reflections on the Medieval Sermon*, edited by Georgiana Donavin and Cary J. Nederman, 157–79. Turnhout: Brepols, 2004.

"Model Building/Structure." British Museum, Collection Online, n.d. https://www.britishmuseum.org/collection/search?keyword=34204.

Monk, Daniel. *An Aesthetic Occupation: The Immediacy of Architecture and the Palestine Conflict*. Durham, NC: Duke University Press, 2002.

Montross, Christine. *Body of Work: Meditations on Mortality from the Human Anatomy Lab*. New York: Penguin, 2007.

Morgan, John. "The Art of Making Anatomical Preparations by Corrosion." *Transactions of the American Philosophical Society* 2 (1786): 366–83.

Morgan, Mary S. *The World in the Model: How Economists Work and Think*. Cambridge: Cambridge University Press, 2012.

Morgan, Mary S., and Margaret Morrison, eds. *Models as Mediators: Perspectives on Natural and Social Science*. Edited by Quentin Skinner. Ideas in Context 52. Cambridge: Cambridge University Press, 1999.

Morrison, Margaret. *Reconstructing Reality: Models, Mathematics, and Simulations*. Oxford: Oxford University Press, 2015.

Nagel, Alexander, and Christopher Wood. *Anachronic Renaissance*. New York: Zone Books, 2010.

Naujokat, Anke. "Ut rhetorica architectura: Leon Battista Alberti's Technique of Architectural Collage." *Candide: Journal for Architectural Knowledge* 2 (2010): 73–100.

Netter, Frank H. *The Ciba Collection of Medical Illustrations: A Compilation of Pathological and Anatomical Paintings*. Summit, NJ: Ciba Pharmaceutical Products, 1948.

Newman, Cathy. "Susan Potter Will Live Forever." In special issue, The Future of Medicine, *National Geographic*, January 2019. https://www.nationalgeographic.com/magazine/2019/01/visible-human-susan-potter-cadaver/.

Noonan, F. Thomas. *The Road to Jerusalem: Pilgrimage and Travel in the Age of Discovery*. Philadelphia: University of Pennsylvania Press, 2007.

"Notes." *Nature* 48, no. 1231 (1893): 107–11.

O'Banion, Patrick J. "Only the King Can Do It: Adaptation and Flexibility in Crusade Ideology in Sixteenth-Century Spain." *Church History* 81, no. 3 (2012): 552–74.

O'Dell, Bob. "RS Tours: Large Outdoor Model of Jerusalem." Root Source: Israeli Jews Teaching Christians Worldwide, 2016. https://www.youtube.com/watch?v=X-kEDKxqRng.

O'Neill, Ynez Violé. "The Fünfbilderserie—A Bridge to the Unknown." *Bulletin of the History of Medicine* 51, no. 4 (1977): 538–49.
Ousterhout, Robert. "Architecture as Relic and the Construction of Sanctity: The Stones of the Holy Sepulchre." *Journal of the Society of Architectural Historians* 62, no. 1 (2003): 4–23.
———. "Is Nothing Sacred? A Modernist Encounter with the Holy Sepulchre." In *On Location: Heritage Cities and Sites*, edited by D. Fairchild Ruggles, 131–50. New York: Springer, 2012.
Pacciani, Riccardo. "Alberti a Firenze. Una presenza difficile." In *Leon Battista Alberti Architetto*, edited by Giorgio Grassi and Luciano Patetta, 211–61. Florence: Banca CR, 2005.
Padan, Yael. *Modelscapes of Nationalism: Collective Memories and Future Visions*. Amsterdam: Amsterdam University Press, 2017.
Paley, William. *Natural Theology; or, Evidences of the Existence and Attributes of the Deity*. 12th ed. London: J. Faulder, [1785] 1809.
Panofsky, Erwin. "Artist, Scientist, Genius: Notes on the 'Renaissance-Dammerung.'" In *The Renaissance: Six Essays*, edited by Erwin Wallace Ferguson, 123–82. New York: Harper & Row, [1953] 1962.
Panofsky, Erwin, and Dora Panofsky. *Pandora's Box: The Changing Aspects of a Mythical Symbol*. Bollingen Series. 2nd ed. New York: Pantheon Books, 1962.
Park, Katharine. "The Criminal and the Saintly Body: Autopsy and Dissection in Renaissance Italy." *Renaissance Quarterly* 47, no. 1 (1994): 1–33.
———. *Secrets of Women: Gender, Generation, and the Origins of Human Dissection*. New York: Zone Books, 2006.
Parliament (United Kingdom). "Cremation Act," 1902.
Patton, George S. *War As I Knew It*. Boston: Houghton Mifflin, 1947.
Peirce, Charles Sanders. *Collected Papers of Charles Sanders Peirce*. 8 vols. Cambridge, MA: Belknap Press of Harvard University Press, 1960.
———. "Lessons of the History of Science." *Commens: Digital Companion to C. S. Peirce*. Helsinki: University of Helsinki: 2003. http://www.commens.org/home.
Perosa, Alessandro, ed. *Giovanni Rucellai ed il suo "Zibaldone."* Vol. 1, *Il Zibaldone quaresimale*. Studies of the Warburg Institute 24. London: Warburg Institute, University of London, 1960, 1981.
Peschard, Isabelle. "Forging Model/World Relations: Relevance and Reliability." *Philosophy of Science* 79 (2012): 749–60.
Piccirillo, Michele. "Miniatura do Santo Sepulchro de Jerusalém." In *Encontro de Culturas: Oito séculos de Missionação Portuguesa*, edited by Maria Natália

Correia Guedes, 86–87. Lisbon: Conferência Episcopal Portuguesa, Mosteiro de S. Vicente de Fora, 1994.

———. *La Nuova Gerusalemme: Artigianato palestinese al servizio dei Luoghi Santi.* Studium Biblicum Franciscanum 51. Bergamo: Velar, 2007.

———. "Un modellino della Basilica del Santo Sepolcro de Gerusalemme conservato a Malta." In *Le vie del Mediterraneo: Relazioni tra Genova e Gerusalemme nel Medioevo e nell'Età Moderna. Atti del convegno internazionale di Genova, 23–24 novembre 1992,* edited by Gabriella Airaldi, 69–83. Genoa: Edizioni culturali internazionali Genova, 1996.

———. "The Role of the Franciscans in the Translation of the Sacred Spaces from the Holy Land to Europe." In *New Jerusalems: Hierotopy and Iconography of Sacred Spaces,* edited by Alexei Lidov, 363–80. Moscow: Indrik, 2009.

Pintore, Angela. "Musical Symbolism in the Works of Leon Battista Alberti: From *De re aedificatoria* to the Rucellai Sepulchre." *Nexus Network Journal* 6, no. 2 (2004): 49–70.

Pontbriand, Vince. "Making Assassin's Creed Unity: Part 3—Assassins in Paris." IGN, YouTube, October 31, 2014. https://www.youtube.com/watch?v=CgcPM9TbhUY.

Popper, Karl. *The Myth of the Framework: In Defence of Science and Rationality.* London: Routledge, 1994.

Portides, Demetris. "How Scientific Models Differ from Works of Fiction." In *Model-Based Reasoning in Science and Technology,* edited by Lorenzo Magnani, 75–87. Studies in Applied Philosophy, Epistemology and Rational Ethics. Berlin: Springer, 2013.

Prawer, Joshua. *The Latin Kingdom of Jerusalem: European Colonialism in the Middle Ages.* London: Weidenfeld and Nicolson, 1972.

Prothero, Stephen. *Purified by Fire: A History of Cremation in America.* Berkeley: University of California Press, 2001.

Rich, Jared. "This Is the Place Where Death Delights to Help the Living." *Academic Medicine* 86, no. 4 (2011): 444.

Richardson, Lewis Fry. *Weather Prediction by Numerical Process.* Cambridge: Cambridge University Press, 1922.

Richardson, Ruth. "Bentham and 'Bodies for Dissection.'" *Bentham Newsletter* 10 (June 1986): 22–33.

Riley-Smith, Jonathan. *Hospitallers: The History of the Order of St. John.* Rio Grande, OH: Hambledon Press, 1999.

Roach, Mary. *Stiff: The Curious Lives of Human Cadavers.* New York: Norton, 2003.

Roberts, K. B., and J. D. W. Tomlinson. *The Fabric of the Body: European Traditions of Anatomical Illustration*. Oxford: Clarendon Press, 1992.

Roeder, Keneth D., and William S. Creighton. "Reports of Sections and Societies: International Union for the Study of Social Insects." *Science*, n.s., 125, no. 3242 (1957): 295–96.

Romera, Raquel, Miguel Ángel Gaertner, Enrique Sánchez, Marta Domínguez, Juan Jesús González-Alemán, and Mario Marcello Miglietta. "Climate Change Projections of Medicanes with a Large Multi-Model Ensemble of Regional Climate Models." *Global and Planetary Change* 151 (2017): 134–43.

Rosner, Lisa. *The Anatomy Murders: Being the True and Spectacular History of Edinburgh's Notorious Burke and Hare and of the Man of Science Who Abetted Them in the Commission of Their Most Heinous Crimes*. Philadelphia: University of Pennsylvania Press, 2009.

Rucellai, Giovanni di Paolo. *Il Zibaldone quaresimale*. Edited by by Alessandro Perosa. Vol. 1 of *Giovanni Rucellai ed il suo "Zibaldone*." Studies of the Warburg Institute 24. London: Warburg Institute, University of London, [1457] 1960.

Ruskin, John. *The Seven Lamps of Architecture*. Mineola, NY: Dover, [1880] 1989.

Russo, Francesco. "The Printed Illustration of Medieval Architecture in Pre-Enlightenment Europe." *Architectural History* 54 (2011): 119–70.

Sappol, Michael. *Dream Anatomy: Exhibition Catalog*. Washington, DC: US Department of Health and Human Services and the National Institutes of Health, National Library of Medicine, 2006.

———. *A Traffic of Dead Bodies: Anatomy and Embodied Social Identity in Nineteenth-Century America*. Princeton, NJ: Princeton University Press, 2002.

Schemmel, Matthias. "Medieval Representations of Change and Their Early Modern Application." *Foundations of Science* 19, no. 1 (2014): 11–34.

Schmidt, Gavin A. "The Physics of Climate Modeling." *Physics Today*, January 2007, 72–73.

Schmitz-Esser, Romedio. *Der Leichnam im Mittelalter: Einbalsamierung, Verbrennung und die kulturelle Konstrucktion des toten Körpers*. Mittelalter-Forschungen. Edited by Bernd Schneidmüller and Stefan Weinfurter. Ostfildern: Jan Thorbecke Verlag, 2014.

Schneider, Stephen H. "Climate Modeling." *Scientific American* 256 (May 1987): 72–80.

Setton, Kenneth Meyer. *The Papacy and the Levant, 1204–1571*. 4 vols. Philadelphia: American Philosophical Society, 1976–84.

Shaftel, Holly, Randal Jackson, and Susan Callery. "Scientific Consensus: Earth's Climate is Warming." In *Global Climate Change: Vital Signs of the Planet*, Earth Science Communications Team at NASA's Jet Propulsion Laboratory, California Institute of Technology, 2018. https://climate.nasa.gov/scientific-consensus/.

Shalev, Zur. *Sacred Words and Worlds: Geography, Religion, and Scholarship.* History of Science and Medicine Library, Scientific and Learned Cultures and Their Institutions 21/2. Mordechai Feingold. Leiden: Brill, 2011.

Shaw, Adrienne. "The Tyranny of Realism: Historical Accuracy and Politics of Representation in Assassin's Creed III." *Loading* 9, no. 14 (2015): 4–24.

Shelton, Don C. "The Emperor's New Clothes." *Journal of the Royal Society of Medicine* 103 (2010): 46–50.

Shen, Yunhe, Jack Norfleet, Zichen Zhao, David Hananel, Daniel Burke, Troy Reihsen, and Robert Sweet. "High-Fidelity Medical Training Model Augmented with Virtual Reality and Conformable Sensors." *Journal of Medical Devices* 10, no. 3 (2016). https://doi.org/10.1115/1.4033847.

Sheppard, F. H. W., ed. *The Parish of St. James Westminster, pt. 2, North of Piccadilly.* Survey of London 31. London: Athlone Press for the Greater London Council, 1963.

Silberman, Neil Asher. *Digging for God and Country: Exploration, Archaeology and the Secret Struggle for the Holy Land.* New York: A. A. Knopf, 1982.

Simmons, Samuel Foart, and John Hunter. *William Hunter: A Memoir.* Glasgow: University of Glasgow Press, [1783] 1983.

Singer, Charles. "A Thirteenth-Century Drawing of the Anatomy of the Uterus and Adnexa." *Proceedings of the Royal Society of Medicine* 9 (November 1915): 43–47.

Skinner, B. F. *Walden Two.* Indianapolis, IN: Hackett, 1948.

Smith, C. F., B. Gami, N. Standfield, and D. C. Davies. "The Role of Anatomy Demonstrators: A Surgical Trainees' Perspective." *Clinical Anatomy* 31 (2018): 409–16.

Spence, D. "Jesper Kyd and Assassin's Creed: Composer Discusses His Work on Ubisoft's Surreal Action Game." IGN Music, 2007, 2009. https://www.ign.com/articles/2007/12/12/jesper-kyd-and-assassins-creed.

Sperling, Christine M. "Leon Battista Alberti's Inscriptions on the Holy Sepulchre in the Cappella Rucellai, San Pancrazio, Florence." *Journal of the Warburg and Courtauld Institutes* 52 (1989): 221–28.

Spiegelhalter, David. *The Art of Statistics: How to Learn from Data.* New York: Basic Books, 2019.

Staby, Ludwig. "A New Epoch in Natural Science: The Earth's Pendulation and Its Effect." *Scientific American supplement 1780* (February 12, 1910): 106.

Stager, Curt. "Sowing Climate Doubt among Schoolteachers: Commentary." *New York Times*, April 27, 2017.

Stephenson, Neal. *Snow Crash*. New York: Bantam, 1992.

Stevenson, William J. *Operations Management*. 13th ed. Boston: McGraw-Hill, 2017.

Stewart, Susan. *On Longing: Narratives of the Miniature, the Gigantic, the Souvenir, the Collection*. Originally published Baltimore, MD: Johns Hopkins University Press, 1984. Durham, NC: Duke University Press, 1993.

Strachey, Lytton. *Eminent Victorians*. London: Penguin, [1918] 1986.

Strauss, Jonathan. *Human Remains: Medicine, Death, and Desire in Nineteenth-Century Paris*. Forms of Living. New York: Fordham University Press, 2012.

Stupart, Frederic. "How a Season Differs from Year to Year: The Rational Causes of Variations in Our Summers and Winters." *Scientific American* supplement 2280 (September 13, 1919): 163.

Sudhoff, Karl. "Abermals eine neue Handschrift der anatomischen Fünfbilderserie." *Archive für Geschichte der Medizin* 3 (1910): 361–66.

———. "Anatomische Zeichnungen aus dem 12. und 13. Jahrhundert." *Studien zur Geschichte der Medizin* 1 (1907): 49–65.

Suppes, Patrick, and Dana Scott. "Foundational Aspects of Theories of Measurement." *Journal of Symbolic Logic* 23, no. 2 (1958): 113–28.

Syson, Luke, Sheena Wagstaff, Emerson Bowyer, and Brinda Kumar. "Life Like: Sculpture, Color, and the Body." Exhibition at the *Met Breuer*. New York: Metropolitan Museum of Art, 2018.

Tarski, Alfred. "A General Method in Proofs of Undecidability." In *Undecidable Theories*, 1–34. Studies in Logic and the Foundations of Mathematics. Amsterdam: Elsevier, 1953.

Tavernor, Robert. *On Alberti and the Art of Building*. New Haven, CT: Yale University Press, 1998.

Taylor, Samuel D. *"Information and Scientific Representation."* MA thesis, Utrecht University, 2015.

Teague, Kevin Anthony, and Nicole Gallicchio. *The Evolution of Meteorology: A Look into the Past, Present, and Future of Weather Forecasting*. Hoboken, NJ: Wiley, 2017.

Thier, Dave. "Ubisoft Is Giving 'Assassin's Creed: Unity' Away for Free to Honor Notre Dame." *Forbes*, April 17, 2019. https://www.forbes.com/sites/davidthier

/2019/04/17/ubisoft-is-giving-assassins-creed-unity-away-for-free-to-honor-notre-dame/#37d775c2ec27.

Thoreau, Henry David. *Walden*. Princeton, NJ: Princeton University Press, [1854] 1971.

Thornton, J. L., and P. C. Want. "Jan van Rymsdyk's Illustrations of the Gravid Uterus Drawn for Hunter, Smellie, Jenty and Denman." *Journal of Audiovisual Media in Medicine* 2, no. 1 (1979): 11–15.

Thurston, Herbert. *The Stations of the Cross: An Account of Their History and Devotional Purpose*. London: Burns and Oates, 1906.

Trachtenberg, Marvin. *Building-in-Time: From Giotto to Alberti and Modern Oblivion*. New Haven, CT: Yale University Press, 2010.

——— . "To Build Proportions in Time, or Tie Knots in Space? A Reassessment of the Renaissance Turn in Architectural Proportions." *Architectural Histories* 2, no. 1 (2014): 1–8.

Trudeau, G. B., and David Levinthal. *Hitler Moves East: A Graphic Chronicle, 1941–1943*. New York: Laurence Miller Gallery, 1989.

Tsafrir, Yoram. "Designing the Model of Jerusalem at the Holy Land Hotel: Hans Zvi Kroch, Michael Avi-Yonah, and an Unpublished Guidebook." *Cathedra: For the History of Eretz Israel and Its Yishuv* 140 (2011): 47–86.

VanOrd, Kevin. "Assassin's Creed Is a Beautiful and Exciting Experience That You'll Remember for Years to Come." *Gamespot*, November 13, 2007. https://www.gamespot.com/reviews/assassins-creed-review/1900-6182793/.

Vasari, Giorgio. "Leon Batista Alberti." Translated by Gaston du C. de Vere. In *Lives of the Most Eminent Painters, Sculptors and Architects*, 10 vols. Vol. 3, 41–49. London: Macmillan, [1568] 1912.

——— . *Le vite de' piú eccellenti architetti, pittori, et scultori Italiani*. Florence: Giunti, 1568.

Venables, Michael. "Exclusive Interview: Ubisoft's Creative Teams on *Assassin's Creed Revelations*." *Wired*, November 3, 2011. http://www.wired.com/geekdad/2011/11/exclusive-interview-ubisofts-creative-teams-on-assassins-creed-revelations/all/.

Vesalius, Andreas. *De humani corporis fabrica libri septem*. Basileae: Ex officina Joannis Oporini, 1543.

——— . *The Fabric of the Human Body: An Annotated Translation of the 1543 and 1555 Editions*. 2 vols. Basel: Karger, 2014.

Vester, Bertha Spafford. *Our Jerusalem: An American Family in the Holy City, 1881–1949*. Garden City, NY: Doubleday, 1950.

Viallet, Ludovic. "The Name of God, the Name of Saints, the Name of the Order: Reflections on the 'Franciscan' Identity During the Observant Period." In *Religious Orders and Religious Identity Formation, ca. 1420–1620: Discourses and Strategies of Observance and Pastoral Engagement*, edited by Bert Roest and Johanneke Uphoff, 132–52. Medieval Franciscans. Leiden: Brill, 2016.

Vikan, Gary. "Ruminations on Edible Icons: Originals and Copies in the Art of Byzantium." In *Studies in the History of Art: Retaining the Original: Multiple Originals, Copies, and Reproductions. Symposium Papers VII*, edited by Henry A. Millon, 47–59. Washington, DC: National Gallery of Art, 1989.

Vincent, Louis-Hugues, and M. Abel. *Jérusalem: recherches de topographie, d'archéologie et d'histoire*. 2 vols. Paris: J. Gabalda for l'Académie des inscriptions et belles-lettres, 1912–26.

von Hilgers, Philipp. "The History of the Black Box: The Clash of a Thing and Its Concept." *Cultural Politics* 7, no. 1 (2011): 41–58.

Wachowski, Lana, and Lilly Wachowski, dir. and authors. *The Matrix*. Warner Bros. Pictures, 1999.

Waldby, Catherine. *The Visible Human Project: Informatic Bodies and Posthuman Medicine*. Biofutures, Biocultures. Edited by Catherine Waldby. London: Routledge, 2000.

Walker, John. *The Autodesk File: Bits of History, Words of Experience*. Thousand Oaks, CA: New Riders, 1989.

Warren, Charles. *The Temple or the Tomb: Giving Further Evidence in Favour of the Authenticity of the Present Site of the Holy Sepulchre, and Pointing Out Some of the Principal Misconceptions Contained in Fergusson's 'Holy Sepulchre' and 'The Temples of the Jews.'* London: Richard Bentley, 1880.

Wartofsky, Marx W. *Models: Representation and the Scientific Understanding*. Edited by Robert S. Cohen. Boston Studies in the Philosophy of Science 48. Dordrecht: Springer Netherlands, 1979.

Weitzmann, Kurt. *Illustrations in Roll and Codex: A Study of the Origin and Method of Text Illustration*. Princeton, NJ: Princeton University Press, 1970.

Weizman, Eyal. *Hollow Land: Israel's Architecture of Occupation*. New York: Verso, 2007.

Welcome to the Garden Tomb. Jerusalem: Garden Tomb Association, n.d. [2019].

Wendler, Reinhard. *Das Modell zwischen Kunst und Wissenschaft*. Paderborn: Wilhelm Fink, 2013.

Wey, William, George Williams, and Bandinel Bulkeley. *The Itineraries of William Wey*. London: J. B. Nichols and Sons, [1458, 1462] 1857.

Wharton, Annabel Jane. *Architectural Agents: The Delusional, Abusive, Addictive Lives of Buildings.* Minneapolis: University of Minnesota Press, 2015.

———. "Doll's House/Dollhouse: Models and Agency." *Journal of American Studies* 53 (2019): 28–56.

———. "Jerusalem's Zions." *Material Religion* 9 (2013): 218–42.

———. "Relics, Protestants, Things." *Material Religion* 10, no. 4 (2014): 412–31.

———. "Scaffold, Model, Metaphor." *ARPA* 4 (May 2016). http://www.arpajournal.net/scaffold-model-metaphor/.

———. *Selling Jerusalem: Relics, Replicas, Theme Parks.* Chicago: University of Chicago Press, 2006.

"What Pause?" *Nature* 545 (May 4, 2017): 6.

Wilkinson, John. *Jerusalem Pilgrimage, 1099–1185.* London: Hakluyt Society, 1988.

Williams, Jonathan, Philip Kevin, Caroline Cartwright, and Jacob Norris. "Sacred Souvenir: the Holy Sepulchre Models in the British Museum." *British Museum Technical Research Journal* 8 (2014): 29–38.

Williams, Kim, and Michael J. Ostwald, eds. *Architecture and Mathematics from Antiquity to the Future. Vol. 1, Antiquity to the 1500s.* Heidelberg: Springer, 2015.

Williamson, John Bruce. *The History of the Temple, London: From the Institution of the Order of the Knights of the Temple to the Close of the Stuart Period.* New York: Dutton, 1924.

Wittgenstein, Ludwig. *Tractatus Logico-Philosophicus.* Translated and edited by C. K. Ogden. International Library of Psychology, Philosophy and Scientific Method. London: Kegan Paul, Trench, Trubner, 1922.

World Health Organization. "Preamble to the Constitution." World Health Organization, 1946. https://www.who.int/governance/eb/who_constitution_en.pdf.

Yang, Xiucheng, Pierre Grussenmeyer, Mathieu Koehl, Hélène Macher, Arnadi Murtiyoso, and Tania Landes. "Review of Built Heritage Modelling: Integration of HBIM and Other Information Techniques." *Journal of Cultural Heritage* 46 (2020): 350–60.

Zamierowski, David S., Kathy A. Carver, and Lawrence E. Guerra. US Patent 9892659B2: Medical Device and Procedure Simulation and Training. Filed January 27, 2017, and issued February 13, 2018.

Zuallart, Giovanni. *Il devotissimo viaggio di Gerusalemme.* Rome: F. Zanetti and Gia Ruffinelli, 1587.

INDEX

Italicized page numbers refer to illustrations.

Acland's Video Atlas of Human Anatomy, 26, 51–52, *52*, 53
Acre, 79, 96
agency, definition, 13–15
Ager, Derek, 1
Alberti, Leon Battista, 4, 66–68, 75–76
Alexandria, Egypt, 3, 23, 30, 53
Amico, Bernardino, 77–83, 90
analog, definition, 37
Angevins of the Kingdom of Sicily and Naples, 79
Anthropocene, definition, 5
Apostle, Leo, 18
Aristotle, 110
Armenians, 55
Assassin's Creed (Ubisoft), 4, 9, 61, 93–100, *95*, *98*
Autodesk (AutoCAD, Revit), 108, 143n20
Avi-Yonah, Michael, 89

Baden-Fuller, Charles, 19
Badiou, Alain, 17
Bagatti, Bellarmino, 79
Baku, Azerbaijan, Heydar Aliyev Center, 105
Bamiyan, Afghanistan, 100
Barbie (Mattel), 1, 13, 20
Bentham, Jeremy, 49–50
Bertolotti, Tommaso, 1
Bethlehem, 74, 84; Church of the Nativity, 79, 80
Bilbao, Guggenheim Museum, 105

BIM (building information modeling), 7, 104–8
Black, Max, 1
black box, definition, 102–4
Bontadino, Giacomo, 33
Brown, Bill, 13
Brown, Dan, 61
Bunge, Mario, 103
Burckhardt, Jacob, 66–67
Burke, William, 45

Callot, Jacques, 77
Carpo, Mario, 76
Casti, John, 17
Cato Institute, 114–15
Charlotte, Queen, 40
Chiara di Montefalco, 30
Christianus, 30
Clarke, Kevin, 17, 18
climate change deniers, 6, 104, 144n49
Columbus, Christopher, 83
commodity model, 10
Conlin, Stephen, 112; "Weather Forecasting Factory," *112*
Constantine, Emperor, 55, 56, 59
Constantinople (Istanbul), Hagia Sophia, 59
Cook, Captain James, 44
Copts, 55
copy, definition, 64
Cosimo II de'Medici, Grand Duke of Tuscany, 83
Counter Reformation, 80
COVID-19, 53, 109

175

Cruikshank, William, 41–42
Crusades, 55, 56, 60, 61, 79, 81, 83, 95, 96

Dalman, Gustaf, 74
Damascus, 96; Great Mosque, 96
Daniel, abbot, 71
de Certeau, Michel, 87
Dee, John, 11
Descartes, René, 110
diagram, definition, 27, 31
discourse, definition, 117–18
Duke University Medical School anatomy lab, 3, 48–49, 52
Durham, Durham Gateway Apartments, *106*

Echenique, Marcial, 20–21
Edington, Wiltshire, Priory of Bonhommes, 71
Eisenman, Peter, 142n15
Elizabeth I, Queen, 110
engraving, 39
Erasmus, Desiderius, 101
Ergas, Henry, 20
European Centre for Medium-Range Weather Forecasts (ECMWF), 113

Fabricius, Johann, 43, 44
Farre, John, 41
Florence, Rucellai tomb, 4, 64–72, *65*, *71*
Franciscan Order, 4, 78–85
Francis of Assisi, 79
Frankfurt, Harry, 115

Gannal, Jean-Nicolas, 43, 48
Garden Tomb Association, 91
Gehry, Frank, 105
Gelfert, Axel, 14
Gilbertus Anglicus, 28
Goodman, Nelson, 7

Gordon, Charles George, 91, 140n99
Greek Orthodox, 55, 80, 84
Guildford, Sir Richard, 61

Hadid, Zaha, 105
Hashashin, 95
Heraclius, Patriarch, 62
Herod the Great, King, 93
Heydenreich, Ludwig, 68–69
Huizinga, Johan, 21
Hunter, William, 37–47, 48, 53; illustration from *Anatomia uteri humani gravidi tabulis illustrata*, *38*

icon, definition, 8–9
index, definition, 9, 31
Intergovernmental Panel on Climate Change (IPCC), 144n52
Israel, West Bank barrier wall, 55
Jerusalem, 54–55; Al-Aksa Mosque, 55; Cenacle, 79, 83; Church of the Holy Sepulchre, 4, 55–56, *56*, *57*, 59, 62, 64, 68–86, *77*, *78*, 90, 93, 97; Dome of the Rock, 9, 55, 93–94, 97; Garden/Gordon's Tomb, 91; Haram al-Sharif/Temple Mount, 86, 94; Herod's Temple, 55, 88; Holy Land Hotel, 89; Israel Museum, 89, 90; Kotel/Wailing Wall, 92; Model of Ancient Jerusalem, 87–93, *88*, 96, 97; Mount Zion, 79, 80, 83, 92; Shrine of the Ascension, 80; "Tomb of David," 92
Jews, 51, 55, 90, 91–93
João V, King, 82
Johnson, Samuel, 11
John Stephen of Calcar, 31–36
Jordanova, Ludmilla, 9
Josephus, Flavius, 89
Justinian, Emperor, 59

Kempe, Margery, 71
Kent, Francis William, 69
Knox, Robert, 45
Knyveton, John, 42, 45, 48
Köprülüzade Fazıl Ahmed Pasha, Grand Vizier, 84
Krautheimer, Richard, 63–64
Kroch, Hans Zvi, 89
Kyd, Jesper, 95

Latour, Bruno, 14, 108
Leonardo da Vinci, 39
Levins, Richard, 17
Levinthal, David, photograph from *Hitler Moves East*, 16, *16*
Lisbon, Vila Viçosa, Holy Sepulchre model (PD/FGB), 82
lithography, 39
London: British Museum, Holy Sepulchre model (BM 10339), 72–86, *73*; Great Windmill Street, William Hunter's School, 42; Royal Academy of Art, 40–41; Royal College of Physicians, 40; Saint George's Hospital, 46; Temple Church, 56–64, *58*, 86

Magnani, Lorenzo, 1
Magni, Cornelio, 81
Mamluks, 79–80
Manet, Édouard, 24
Maria Theresa, Empress, 82
Meurent, Victorine, 24
Miousse, Caroline, 98
molecular model, glass, 116, *117*
Morgan, John, 41
Morgan, Mary, 19, 20
Morrison, Margaret, 14, 20
Muslims, 95
Mussolini, Benito, 87
Mylne, Robert, 42

New Haven, Yale College of Medicine, 45
New York: General Motors' Futurama, World's Fair, 1939, 87; World Trade Center, 87

Orlando, Holy Land Experience, 91
Ottomans, 80–84, 92
Oxford, Bodleian Library, Ashmole 399, 25–30, *26*, *29*, 53, 59

Paley, William, 37
Palmyra, Temple of Bel, 100
Pandora, 5, 101–2
Patton, George S., 110
Paul II, Pope, 72
Paul III, Pope, 84
Peirce, Charles, 37, 72
Peschard, Isabelle, 17
Peter the Hermit, 83
Phillips, Alban William Housego, 3
Phillips-Newlyn Hydraulic Analogue Machine, 2, 3
Popper, Karl, 17
Powell, Colin, 83
Primo, David, 17, 18
Protestant, 50, 79–83, 90–91, 93

recension, definition, 27–28
Reformation, 80
relic, definition, 85–86
Richard I, King, 94
Richardson, Lewis Fry, 111–12
Ridolfi, Andreas, Auxiliary Bishop of Constantinople, 84
Roman Catholics, 51, 61, 74, 79–80, 90
Rome: Museo della Civiltà Romana, Model of Constantine's Rome, 87; Old Saint Peters, 60
Rucelli, Giovanni di Paolo, 66, 68, 69, 71
Rymsdyk, Jan van, 38–39, 45

Salah ad-Din, Sultan, 94
Santiago de Compostela, cathedral, 60
Schmidt, Gavin, 114
Schneider, Stephen H., 116–17
Scientific American, 113
Scott, Sir Walter, 61
Shakespeare, William, 10–11
simulacrum, definition, 51
Skinner, Burrhus Frederic, 116
Sloane, Hans, 77
souvenir, definition, 85–86
Staby, Ludwig, 113
Strange, Robert, 38–39, 45
strong and weak models, definition, 12
Stuart, John, 3rd Earl of Bute, 46
symbol, definition, 8–9

Tavenor, Robert, 69
Templar Order, 4, 61, 95
Theophanes, 30
Thoreau, Henry David, 116
Titus Flavius Vespasianus, 88
Trent, Council of, 84
Tsafrir, Yoram, 89

Valetta, Malta, Monastery of St. Ursula, Holy Sepulchre model, 82
van Butchell [Burchell], Martin, 42
Vasari, Giorgio, 66–67
Venables, Michael, 99
Vesalius, Andreas, 23, 31–36, 41, 45, 46, 53; frontispiece and illustrations from *De humani corporis fabrica libri septem*, 33, 36
Vienna, Kunsthistorisches Museum, Holy Sepulchre model, 82, 139n90
Visible Human Project, 51
Vitruvius, 11, 86
von Hagens, Gunther, 41

Warren, Charles, 91
Wartofsky, Marx, 1, 8
Weizman, Eyal, 54
Wendler, Reinhard, 1
Western Union, 111
Wey, William, 71
Whitefield, George, 50
Wittgenstein, Ludwig, 101

Zoffany, Johann, 40